Dream A Difference

First published in 2019
by Rosetta Life and Dream a Difference
London, UK

Designed and typeset by Country Setting,
Kingsdown, Kent CT14 8ES

Printed in England by Short Run Press,
Exeter EX2 7LW

A CIP record for this book is available from the British Library

ISBN 978-1-9998488-4-2

Dream a Difference

Poetry Anthology
2019

www.dreamadifference.art

A map of partnership locations

Hawes School, Yorkshire

Cotswold & Chadlington Schools

Oxfordshire Hospital School

Dartington Primary School, & Charter School, London

Devon

Grizzly Hill + Washington Ridge, Schools, Nevada County

Al Farah, Damascus

Prep B School, Gaza

Compassionate Care, Korail, Dhaka

Bondeko Refugee Settlement, Kampala

Island Hospice, Harare

Prince Edward Secondary School, Harare

WordnSound Collective, Johannesburg

Sunflower Hospice, Bloemfontein

ACKNOWLEDGMENTS

I would like to thank all the poets and teachers who have worked tirelessly to support new ways of bringing creative writing into the classroom, and all the librarians and IT support staff who have made the Skype workshops happen so seamlessly. Particular thanks are due to Kate Clanchy, who took the time to write some wonderful 'how to write' resources for the schools participating in the project. We thank the Arts Council of England and the Ronald Duncan Foundation for supporting the financial development of the project and Nevada County Arts Council for supporting its development in USA.

Many people who have been critical to the development of the project are unrecognised in the anthology: Manas Ghanem for helping us secure the partnership with Al Farah Choir of Joy in Syria, Heba Ghanem for her translations of Arabic into English and English into Arabic, Claire Morris for helping to secure the partnership in Bangladesh, Joan Marston for introducing me to the African Palliative Care Association and Johmary Ssekate for nurturing the partnership in Uganda.

More personally, I would like to thank the many friends and colleagues who have offered their time and support to help find the right way for the project to thrive, Francesca Beard, Jo Crudge, Karina Moreton, Chris Redmond and Eliza Tudor, and particular thanks are due to my partner Chris Rawlence.

Most significantly, I would like to thank my three greatest teachers – the three children who inspired the idea for the project: Bobby, Grace and Anna Jarrett Rawlence.

Lucinda Jarrett, Artistic Director *Rosetta Life*

CONTENTS

CONTINUED

COLOUR ILLUSTRATIONS

FOREWORD

by Baroness Ilora Finlay of Llandaff and
Caroline Heath-Taylor

This anthology of short poems takes us through the eyes of children from across the world, as they navigate complex human issues and experiences. Despite vast circumstantial and cultural differences in the lives of these young authors, these poems find the points of convergence in human experience and celebrate them in a way which harnesses a child's openness and enthusiasm to reach out to others.

This initiative by *Dream a Difference* has given an invaluable space for children to share their experiences of grief, pain and trauma and to express it in a form which is both cathartic for the poet and which expands the understanding and empathy of its readers. Through sharing, these children can experience the global community and know they are not alone. In this anthology we all confront failures of social justice and the abuse of human rights. Amongst the diverse tones and stylistic differences of these poems there is, undoubtedly, a common voice with a plea for readers to peel away any scales of prejudice and see the beauty of diversity. These poems are also charged with an infectious excitement as they speak of hope for a world founded on second chances, tolerance, kindness – a place where, whatever their differences, every person is free to know love and harmony.

Our allegiances to poetry are formed by our first few readings or, indeed, the first few lines we scribble on a piece of lined school paper. By addressing such profound issues early on in their education, I hope that these young poets will cling to these issues and allow them to seep into their more sophisticated verse as they nurture their creativity in the future. This collection exemplifies the continued relevance of poetry for building cross-cultural relationships - for poetry touches something deep within us and, because of that, enriches our dealings with the world.

INTRODUCTION

by Lucinda Jarrett

*I am not an Athenian or a Greek,
but a citizen of the world.*
SOCRATES

Welcome to the second poetry anthology from the *Dream a Difference* team. When we published the first in 2017, there were only four participating schools and three participating countries – England, Zimbabwe and Palestine. Two years later and we are managing partnerships in ten countries between sixteen schools and informal learning centres. These include Uganda, South Africa, Bangladesh, Brazil, Syria, the United States of America and Greece. This pioneering project has grown rapidly and this anthology celebrates the richness of these exchanges.

Dream a Difference nurtures global citizenship through poetry. The concept is not new. Long before texts and e-mail, pen pal exchanges initiated and supported language skills development across Europe. James Berardi, who directs a small school in rural North California, passionately recounts the pen pal exchange his family had encouraged with a young girl from Chernobyl, which had led to her spending time with his family every summer. Last year he was in Russia for her marriage. This rich encounter was facilitated by the American Field Service (AFS) Intercultural Programs – an international youth exchange organization. In James' words, 'the AFS programme was established after the war. I guess they reckoned if kids got to know each other, they would not point a gun at each other'.

Dream a Difference is unique in that it specifies the written exchanges should take place through poetry. We choose poetry as a form because it enables children and young people to focus on the emotional and sensory experiences the children describe instead of the structures of narrative and story. The emotional heartland of writing poetry enables young people to share life experiences that might previously have been seen as having nothing in common. Shared poetry exchanges open windows on other cultures in a world that is crying out for mutual understanding.

The immediacy of Skype exchanges have been a vital means of achieving this. A Skype open mic session enables young people to read poems directly to each other, meet their authors, and ask questions about each other's lives. I remember the first time this happened, in an exchange between Palestine and The Cotswold School in the UK, when young Palestinians asked to meet particular young people who had written to them. 'Is Aggie there?' one girl shouted through Skype, 'Thank you so much for your beautiful poem'. Blushing, the English girl came to the screen where the Palestinian girls complimented her poetry and thanked her for her messages of hope. A deeply moving exchange followed. The English children offered the deer as an image of hope, but the Palestinian children saw the deer as a creature that ran away, and preferred the image of a butterfly, but this was too fragile as an image of hope for the English children. Finally both Palestinians and English agreed that hope might be best symbolised by the image of a shaft of light through a half open door.

Over the past two years, Skype sessions like this have become increasingly important to the success of *Dream a Difference*. In the course of a recent exchange between a Buckinghamshire Primary School and Korail Slum in Dhaka, Bangladesh, we invited both parties to pause and think about how they might explore the challenging themes of gender, class and disability discrimination that had been raised in the Bangladeshi poetry manifesto. One girl from Buckinghamshire wrote, 'I hear the sound of the water singing, come sing with us, seize the power within'. From Korail Slum, a group of twenty children responded by choreographing a dance which they performed via Skype. The Buckinghamshire school children were amazed as the brightly coloured clothes of the Bangladeshi girls traced their bodies turning in a rising wave of energy and joy. On another occasion, a storm had broken the Skype link, so for one hour the students could not get online. The English students at London's Charter School used this down time to write a collective *Praise Poem for Zimbabwe*. In Uganda, a young person from a refugee settlement wrote a poem called *Fish! My Hero*, telling us how his school fees were paid and his uncle's life was saved because his grandmother could sell fish that his father caught in the lake. English primary school children were shocked to hear that securing a school place was dependent of the size of a fish catch, but were amused when the Ugandans showed how the art of fishing could be learnt using a stick as a rod and a piece of string as the line.

There are significant dilemmas for an editor when presented with several hundred poems from young people around the world. How do you avoid overwhelming the reader with the sheer number of poems? What criteria do you bring to bear on your selection? Since this is a volume dedicated to empowering children through making their voices heard, I have opted for poems with the strongest individual voices. Some poems are published in translation, others are published in the original Arabic and also in translation, and others are from young people who are writing in English where English is their second or third language. I have not edited or changed any of the poems and hope that their strength lies in the diversity of the voices of the collection.

In discussing the project, some people have told me that it is futile to expect young people from primary schools to be able to relate to stories of child labour, refugees fleeing war, experiences of bereavement and conflict. I have wrestled with this myself, but after three years of leading *Dream a Difference*, I have come to the conclusion that children will empathise with these issues if they are introduced to them sensitively. When children are encouraged to share their curiosity and feelings about these themes in peer led exchanges, there is a real possibility for enlightenment and understanding. Understanding a complex issue in a poem written by one child to another, creates a burning desire for communication. The poetry in this collection is testament to the creativity that is awakened by empathy.

Lucinda Jarrett, March 2019

CALIFORNIA, USA
Twin Ridges School District, Nevada County

Introduction

by Kirsten Casey

In America, we formed a partnership with Nevada County Arts Council on the Western Slope of the Sierra Nevada Mountains in California. Nevada County Arts Council helped us identify two isolated schools within Twin Ridges, one of the smallest school districts in the United States. Nevada County Arts Council's teaching poets: Kirsten Casey and Conrad Cecil, have been working with students at Grizzly Hill and Washington Schools.

'Dear You' poems

This group of poems was written by eighth graders at Grizzly Hill school. The poems are in epistolary form, meaning they are written in the style of a letter. The inspiration for their work is the idea that there are children, just like them across the world, who share more similarities with them than differences. What if they are writing to a version of themselves, in a place that may be foreign, but through the feelings that they each possess? This is the result . . .

Dear You,
By Ariel, Grizzly Hill, 8th grade

We share the same feeling, hope of living another day.
The hope to be free
like a bird to fly to our dreams.
We share the same anger, a twisting, turning hole
in our heads, dark and wet, alone.
Alone with no love, no home, no hearth to sleep by.
Completely alone, like a little stone
on the surface of the sand.

We share the same smells,
drops of rain falling on our faces,
the smell of the world
fills us up and awakens our senses.

Dear You,
By Sophie, Grizzly Hill, 8th grade

Do we share the same ground? Is it cool and calming?
Does it go between your toes, is it a carpet of green grass?
Does its earthy scent fill you upward,
lift you into the blue sky,
are you happy with your feelings?

Dear You,
By Alia, Grizzy Hill, 3–5th grade

We share the same fog,
like a blanket of warmth covering a tiny, young child
with red hair, sitting outside his house shivering,
until a nice grandmother comes to make him warm.

We feel the same hope,
like a single candle burning bright to light
the path of a tired, withered old man
who escaped from captivity to find his granddaughter.

We taste the same white goat's milk.
like the bright glowing moon, sprinkled
with fresh maple sugar.

We hear the same crackling fires,
like the crunch of black pebbles underneath
a dark brown boot, with a sole as thick as the earth.
We smell the same water,
as clear and clean as just washed glass
of an apartment building thirteen stories high.

We wish for the same happiness,
like a plum tree blossom in early April,
with a fairy with no worries nestled inside of it.

Dear You,

By Elysia, Grizzly Hill, 8th grade

We share the same stars, shining as bright
as a lake with sun reflecting, in little beams of light.
We share the same fears, being unimportant, forgotten.
We see the sun climb high into the sky, resting
on its throne of light and warmth.
We see the same sun dipping back into the depths,
leaving a trail of red and purple streaks,
like a painter using the sky as its canvas.
We smell the same morning air, with its freshness,
like a cold winter day with glittering snow
falling quietly.

HARARE, ZIMBABWE
Island Hospice

Introduction

By Val Maasdorp, Island Hospice

Island Hospice and Healthcare (Island) have been partnering for many years with the Zimbabwe Government and communities to provide psycho-social support for children who have lost either one or both parents. The HIV / AIDS pandemic has resulted in some children having responsibility of caring for ill parents or relatives at home. This, in turn prevents them from fully experiencing and enjoying their childhood. Orphans and vulnerable children in Zimbabwe experience grief compounded by poverty, by limited access to resources, services, education, and at times, neglect by guardians.

Island Programmes for Orphans and Vulnerable Children

The programmes designed for young carers and bereaved children aim to promote loss adjustment, coping and resilience – in turn resulting in reduced vulnerabilities.

The *Dare to Dream a Difference* workshop wished to acknowledge and work with the children's challenges by providing a supportive environment for them to express their feelings and share experiences. The children came together and through play, drawings, poetry, letter writing and discussion, began to open up, share their experiences and to express their feelings. Island continues to run psychosocial support activities for vulnerable children in the community, understanding that these programmes need to be an ongoing process towards healing.

Dear You,

My Many Wishes

By Ayanda, aged 12

I am in cloud nine writing to you about myself and my
wishes
I am a girl of your age
I have so many wishes,

Wishing to be a jeweller
Wishing I was a tree
Wishing I was a school.

As a jeweller,
I would collect lots of jewellery
Old and new
Redesign it into a marvellous piece.

As a tree,
 I would be so useful to people
I would provide oxygen,
I would provide firewood and timber
In the villages, people would depend on me.
As a school,
Children would come and learn
To have a better and brighter future
To learn other foreign languages
Oh how very rewarding.
I wish I could visit your country,
See you for the first time.
Tell you all about myself
Tell you all about my beloved country Zimbabwe.

A Song for My Family

By Tariro, aged 12

Dear you, I write to tell you about my family
Who live in a country called Zimbabwe
In the capital city called Harare
In a location called Mabvuku.

Dear You
Thank you for writing'
This is My family'
'My very precious family.'

I lost my mother when I was a child,
My uncles, aunts, nieces and nephews
 Are always there for me
They console and take care of me,

'My family'
'My very precious family.'

I wish to have a family of my own
My own children and grand children
I would love them more than anything in the world
I would give them all the love that I have.

Dear You
Thank you for writing'
This is My family'
'My very precious family.'

A family of my own would be so important to me
I would love to rely on my own children
I would love to shower them with all the blessings
And shower them with unconditional love,

'My family'
'My very precious family'.

Our Dreams Will Never Die

*Our dreams will never die, is a collective poem written
by young people at Island Hospice Zimbabwe, aged 12–14*

Living under the heat of the same sun,
Raised under different circumstances
Having encountered multiple losses,
Accidents, illnesses, and violence.

Expressing the same emotions,
Having similar surroundings,
Buildings, vegetation, people,
We all have similar and different dreams to work on.

Dreams of a career, want to be a doctor or a pilot?
Being the best footballer in your country?
Want to run your own companies?
Whatever we want to be, that's our dream.

No matter how many losses, our dreams will not die,
Parents have died, years have gone by,
But their memories remain alive in our hearts,
And give us the strength and hope for tomorrow.

We forever cherish the short life we shared,
Periods and seasons of pain might come,
Painful feelings and emotions might be triggered,
But our dreams live on.

Come what may, our dreams will never die,
No matter what might happen,
We shall pursue our dreams,
Our dreams, our dreams, our dreams.

DEVON, ENGLAND
Dartington Primary School

Dartington Primary School is a primary school based in Totnes, Devon, England. Their partner was the literary collective of spoken word artists, Wordnsound, based in Johannesburg, South Africa.

Workshop Poet:

Chris Redmond

Chris Redmond has been working with Dartington School for three years. He is a spoken word artist, educator and producer working with cross-art form collaboration. He is artistic director of *Tongue Fu* – the UK's leading spoken word and music show. He is passionate about the arts and bringing people together to experience, think and feel collectively and has led three cycles of workshops for *Dream a Difference*. This selection of poems was written between September 2017 and July 2018.

Dear You,
By Milo, aged 10

Even though you live on the other side, we share a lot.
We share feelings and emotions, when our tears drop
To the dusty ground, splashing quietly.
We share happiness when our smiles are so big they
almost hit our ears.

We share the same earth, sun and moon,
The sunburn boiling our red noses,
The puddles splashing up in our wellie boots
And the dirty water seeping through our socks,
We share the same rainclouds in the sky,
The hope that the rain won't come.

When we roll out of bed and the sun rises
We all start a new day.
When the sun sets we all
Feel the same happiness of the beauty and the views.

Even though you live on the other side, we share a lot.

My Amazing Trousers
By Zach, aged 10–11

My amazing trousers are made of bubbles and clouds,
Smell like a bubble bath,
Sound like a waterfall,
Can stop global warming,
Can save the sea
Could stop wars
Are awesome to me.

My Amazing Trousers
By Sol, aged 10–11

My Amazing Trousers are made of macaroni cheese
They are soft and siky and put on with ease.
My amazing trousers are spat on by llamas,
They are just as cosy as fluffy pyjamas.
I feed the homeless, I feed the poor
And if they ask, I'll give them more.
I'll come round town breakfast, lunch and dinner
To make every human feel like a winner.

My Amazing Trousers
By Silvia, aged 10–11

My amazing trousers
They are made of stars
And some days they decide
To fly me to Mars

My amazing trousers
They smell like bonfire smoke
And they don't react kindly
If you give them a poke

My amazing trousers,
They give food to the hungry,
And money to the poor
And if you ask for more
Oh yes, they will give you more

Me and my amazing trousers
One day we will save the world.

Dear You,
By Joshua, aged 10

I wonder if your mornings are like mine,
A boiled egg and butter soldiers,
Cars zooming by,
Looking at the sky,
Thinking why can't time go by.

After school is a blast,
Playfighting on the grass:
Happy to be here,
Happy to be home.

My Amazing Trousers
By James, aged 10–11

My amazing trousers taste like cheesy cheese
My amazing trousers look like a butter sausage
My amazing trousers feel like a space cow eating cheesy
cheese riding a butter sausage
My amazing trousers sound like a salmon wrestling a
dinosaur eating fermented wellies
My amazing trousers smell like an electric urchin
chewing scissors on a cliff
My amazing trousers can teleport, change the future and
shape shift.
My amazing trousers.

My Amazing Trousers

By Lily, aged 10–11

My amazing trousers,
Purple and blue and red,
Soft and silky,
Satin and lace,
Embroidered and perfectly stitched.

My amazing trousers.
They are thermal,
They never tear,
Or ever get dirty
Never ever stain.

They make me popular,
Girls ask where I got them,
Boys ask me to hang out,
I make countless friends,
Get good grades too,
I love my magic trousers
But why or why am I not content?

I went to the shops today
To pick up some food for my Mum,
A man sat outside the shops
A shopping bag, a mug
That was all he had.
That was all he owned
This man,
This human,
With two things of his
To call his own.

I walked past him,
The bell of the shop tinkled
I bought my goods
And proceeded to the door,
The bell,
The man,
Guilt, guilt guilt
Overwhelming guilt.

Mum gave me
The exact money
I would need for the food.
She said not to spend it
On anything else,
But still I didn't help him,
Didn't offer him a meal
Or even a coffee.

How can I live with myself
Knowing I didn't throw
Every last penny
In my pocket at him?
How can I live?
We locked eyes,
In that moment
I saw his pain,

How can I live?
Bur more importantly,
How can he?

My Amazing Trousers

By Charlie, aged 10–11

My amazing trousers are made of silk
My amazing trousers smell like roses.
My amazing trousers are magical.
They take me around the world,
Showing every detail,
Helping other people.

My amazing trousers taste like chocolate,
My amazing trousers
Can make anything possible.
My amazing trousers would cure cancer
My amazing trousers would leave nobody hungry.

My amazing trousers would help the homeless
To get a job and a house
My amazing trousers,
How I wish you were real!

JOHANNESBURG, SOUTH AFRICA

WordnSound Live Literature Movement

Introduction

by Mutinta Bbenkele, WordnSound

The reality of reading and writing is a luxury in the South African context. The ever fluctuating levels of education and ineffective measures of teacher training truly put the country at a disadvantage. But our nation is built on an oral tradition. Young and old flourish in the light of this intrinsic skill. I have ventured into the city centre of Johannesburg where I was able to interact with a rather curious group of refugee children, who form a part of two after-school programs. These are the pieces they came up with.

Happy

By Jonathan

I want to be happy
Like the sea
Like a sunny day
Like a bird learning to fly
I want to be happy
For my mum
For my dad
For my baby brother
I am on my way to happy

Dancing

By Magdeline

Dancing is my body, moving to the world's music
The music is fast then slow
Music is happy and sad
Dancing is funny sometimes
I can't tell my feet what to do when they listen to music
My hands play with the air
The music will never stop

Uganda

By Jean-Luke

Where I come from we have forests of animals
Gorillas that beat their chest trying to be stronger than lions
We have great mango juice and our fields have many fruits
We are blacker than soil but brighter than the sun and that can not be undone
We have tall people, short people, and straight people and round people
We have angry men and quiet men
We have loud women and calm women
We have all the colours of the rainbow on our clothes
But now
Home is a thorn
Home is a dark memory
Home is a thing I must forget

Death is

By Andre

(Response to Penelope Chanter's 'Death Is')

A vacant void
A painful cry
A dying thing
An unanswered question
A unwelcome visitor who sits with me at night

Mom

By Ujoma

Tall. Brave. Pretty. Smells nice.
Thank you for always holding my hand
And kissing me goodnight
I love your fufu
I love all of your food

Favourite

By Khumbulani

I have a red wheel barrow
It was my Christmas present
I take it wherever I go
I never want to see my wheel barrow go into the dustbin

Lonely

By Nothemba

I get lonely waiting for my sister to finish with school
She is in grade 9
I talk to myself and think about what to say to her when
she comes
I can't wait to be in grade 9
I want to jump in the sky and bring her a star
But I am only 9

My House

By Angelo

My house is small and warm
You must visit in winter
The dust stays on the floor because there is no wind
It is shiny on the outside
You can always smell the food
My house is small like a matchbox

I Want a Puppy

By Sandra

(Response to Sanchia's 'Love is both Genders')

I want a puppy that will grow into a dog
And when it is a dog it will be my best friend
Mum always asks, what will it eat
I want to feed him chocolate
His name is Frank
Like my dad
My dog is like a wish that I really want to have

Fun

By Makgotso

Fun is playing in the street
Running around until you sweat
Fun is my skirt, dancing in the wind
Fun is church
Fun is like a rainbow after the rain
You know it is somewhere

DHAKA, BANGLADESH

In Bangladesh, we formed an alliance with Compassionate Care Korail, a palliative care initiative based in **Korail Slum, Dhaka**. An amazing project co-ordinator, Khadija Shopna took on the project management of *Dream a Difference* in Dhaka.

Introduction

by Professor Nezamuddin Ahmad,
Director of Compassionate Care, Korail

Initially, it seemed a huge challenge to meet the needs of Korail slum, the largest slum in Bangladesh, accommodating around one hundred and forty thousand dwellers. We found out that there are one hundred and fifty two informal education centres/schools, each accommodating 100 to 300 students, mostly from class (grade) one to class five, few up to class eight. Most of them are between the age 5 to 13. We calculated that there would be around two thousand children going to these centers and we wanted to include all of them.

We arranged an inter school art, poetry and essay writing competition on the theme of how do we dream our world to be and there was a huge response: 117 artworks, 60 poems and 75 essays!

The winning poems were published online and a small group of children and young people were invited to a series of art and poetry workshops led by poet and videographer, Nazmul Huda.

We Want a World

By Bani

We want a world
Where we can have a mother's love.
We want a world
Where we can have sweet dreams.
We want a world
Where trust is possible
We want a world
Where there is no jealousy between us,
We want a world
Where we can see the light of an education
We want a world
Where there is no sound, but the crooning
of a mother's lullaby
We want a world
Where happiness comes from our sorrows
We want a world
Where we have freedom in our country

The World of Our Dreams
By Sarna

We want a world
Where there is no shadow of discrimination.

We will stand together
Men and women, adults and children

In this world of our dreams.
Child labour will stop.

We will stand together by dreaming
While the stars are plentiful in the sky.

By carrying the dream
We might be able to start out on our journey.

Today we stretch out our fingers, hold out our hands
We open ourselves to our dreams.

My Dream Land
By Samia, aged 10

If this country could be
Like my dreamland,
Where all the people are smiling
And have forgotten violence.
I wish this country were a place of peace,
Where our only experience is love.

Ah, if only my country would
Be the land in my mind.

Tree of Life

By Sourov, aged 11

Our environment could be so beautiful
If we could only plant more trees.

The tree is a familiar friend;
Its blossom and its oxygen
Nurturing our lives!
Birds sing sweetly from the treetops
Childhood fun is hanging from the branches.

Those who are cutting down trees
Causing the deforestation,
Polluting the environment-
Can't you understand that this is wrong?
Life and trees have a strong relationship.

Environment Pollution

By Shorna, aged 12

Dirt and rubbish filling up
Our loving land;
Rivers-canals getting polluted
Are harming our environment.

Inhabited homes, streets and roads
We shall keep always clean;
In this way we can surely make
A pollution-free, happy Bangladesh.

Labourer

By Forhad, aged 13

In this beautiful world
The real builders
Do not get our full appreciation.

All the beautiful structures and things around us,
The labourers who built upon this ground,
Why they are neglected today?

As the labourers drooped in sweat,
This country has been developed,
But I say to the people of this society
Why are labourers not respected?

We All

By Lamia, aged 12

The Pakistani invading forces
Took away uncounted lives
Took away the voices
Took away our songs.

Bangla is my voice
Bangladesh is my heart

So we made a promise
To love Bangladesh,
We fought for this land
All together we stand.

A further selection of poems from Dartington
Primary School in England.

Introduction

by Elsie and Seran

The *Dream a Difference* project is an amazing project that involves children all over the world. We have loved writing poems as it is a way of expressing yourself through words. Chris has shared poems with us from other children across the globe. They made us think lots about the issues these children have faced and how lucky we are. We were surprised at how things that seem small to us, such as fish, were so important to them.

Happiness

by Beau, aged 9

Happiness is a sweet bear
Happiness wears a big long fluffy brown bear coat
Happiness has a big smile
Happiness lives in a small blue cottage
Happiness's pet is a tiny German short haired pointer, called Molly
Happiness loves all people.

Fun

by Reuben, aged 9

Fun is a man, bright as the sky,
he is big and strong and fast,
Fun is funny and happy,
Fun surfs and skates,
Fun's voice is dark and deep
and Fun is very, very handsome.
Fun is everywhere.

My Grandad

by Elsie, aged 10

A loving, hugging machine,
A crazy clever clogs,
A thoughtful, silly figure,
He made lovely mac and cheese.

If We Ruled the World!!

by George, aged 9

We would:
Ban war
Make a home for everyone
Make all dogs, cats and birds never die
until they reach forty five human years
Ban cancer
Give everyone a superpower
Ban all weapons
Put wifi everywhere – literally everywhere -
the range would be legendary
Ban sweets
Wipe memories of those who know what sweets really
are

Ban Brexit forever
Stop Trump

Boris

by Daniel, aged 10

My friend Boris
funny laugher
sleeping lion player

My friend Boris
sand cake baker
bike buddy

My friend Boris
'you're it' chaser
fun house builder

What is Love?

**By Hannah's Class, ages 8–10,
Dartington Primary School**

Love's the Mayor of Lovesville
It's a lovely town
Love's smile is a rainbow
half up and half down

Love is all genders
They wear anything they please
a pink dress, with red hearts, green sandals,
a cowboy hat and ripped jeans

One eye is a storm
the other is an orange sun
Love loves to dance
And will dance with anyone

Love is happy, love is kind
Love is yours and love is mine
Love is me and love is you
Love has got so much to do

Love walks slowly
swaggering with the breeze
They love to knock on doors and hug people
And plant flowers for the bees

Love rides a horse
and throws a lasso
Love loves nothing more than saying
I love you

One eye is a storm
the other is an orange sun
Love loves to dance
And will dance with anyone

Love is happy, love is kind
Love is yours and love is mine
Love is me and love is you
Love has got so much to do

Love drives a red corvette
they fly a private jet
they bake cakes
the best cakes you can get
they have pets you won't believe
like chihuahuas and baboons
with heart-shaped bums
that toot marvellous tunes

Love knows sometimes
it's OK to be sad
Could tame a raging bull
With love in their hands
Love can heal cracks
in buildings and hearts
When you let love in
The magic can start

Love is happy, love is kind
Love is yours and love is mine
Love is me and love is you
Love has got so much to do

Fear is . . .
by Elsie, aged 10

a tiny scared girl
who hides whenever shadows loom
sneaks through alley-ways not to be seen,
sits alone away from you and me
and doesn't trust anyone.

Fear is . . .
by Seran, aged 9

A thin little seven year old spirit
wearing a knee length blue-grey dress
with white short mouse brown hair
in a side parting with one clip in
and big brown eyes,
who hides under the covers
and behind boxes at night-fall.

OXFORDSHIRE, ENGLAND
Chadlington Primary School

A partnership with *Bondeko Refugee Settlement, Uganda*

Introduction

We set up a partnership exchange between Chadlington Primary School and Bondeko Refugee Settlement.

Chadlington Primary School is a small village primary school in the heart of West Oxfordshire. It is set in the Evenlode valley and is on the edge of the Cotswolds. The project was run for children aged 10 –11years in years 5 and 6. The children shared their dreams, learnt about the challenges faced by the refugee children and shared poems of support and shared understanding.

Bondeko Refugee Livelihoods Center (Bondeko Center), is a nationally-registered, refugee-led organization founded by refugees in 1997 to support those fleeing violence in the Democratic Republic of Congo (DRC). Bondeko Centre supports impoverished, often traumatized refugees, especially women and children, who reach Uganda's capital in Kampala without connections or aid. It is a community centre for both refugees and local Ugandans, as well as an emergency shelter for refugees.

My Dream
By Bobby, aged 9

What if you were in an enormous stadium
With millions and millions of people?
There is total silence all around you,
The keys are communicating with you,
You need to start making a sound,
Your legs are shaking like jelly;
Your fingers are starting to move,
The piano is making a noise,
The keys are making sense,
The crowd is roaring louder,
Now I'm crowded with feelings of joy.
My dream is to be a concert pianist.

What is yours?

What Are Your Dreams?
By Jake, aged 9

I want to be a writer who is popular
One with imagination and dreams of fame

I want to create imaginative books
With beautiful pictures full of detailed drawings.

My books will give people hope
So that no one ever gives up.

My Dream
By Sam, aged 10

Monitors, computers, printers, copies
All in IT
My deepest wish, my dearest ambition,
Is to work in IT.

Monitors that won't turn on,
Computers that overheat,
Printers that won't print a thing
Copiers that jam.

Never fear,
Because I'm here
And I do IT

What is Your Dream?
By Imogen, aged 10

You could be an author,
A firefighter or a horse rider,
Or a palaeontologist or even a magician.
I have a few tricks up my sleeve.
So do as I say and dream big,
You just have to start somewhere.

My Dream
By Cameron, aged 10

My dream is to join the Royal Armoured Corp
Which I could not do before
Because I had a heart condition.
It really changed my position:
I wanted to become an officer
Or maybe just a sergeant;
The main thing is that I could not
Because of my faulty heart.
But now at last there is hope
And my dream is no longer without a will
Or a way

KAMPALA, UGANDA
Bondeko Refugee Settlement

Poems written by refugee children at Bondeko Refugee Setlement, Kampala to children in UK primary schools:

Fish
By Kerene

Fish, Fish, Fish
You are so great!
You are my hero!

My grand mother sells Fish
My mother sells Fish
All to get money and pay my school fees

Fish, Fish, Fish
Fish is my Hero
You saved my uncle from death
He was poisoned but mummy sold Fish
The money saved my uncle
Fish you are so great
Fish you are my Hero.

To Kerene, Fish My Hero
By Bobby, aged 9

I have fish, you have fish
I buy fish, you catch fish.
Splash, splish, splosh.
Salmon, trout, cod and haddock
We can name them all.
All fish comes easily to us,
We buy it in packets from supermarkets,
You have to catch it from running water,
Splish, splash, splosh.
I'm glad fish saved your uncle,
I'm glad fish saved your education.
Build your own supermarket one day
And sell fish to more people.
Splish, spash, splosh.
I have fish, you have fish,
I buy fish, you catch fish.
.

To Kerene: Who Would Have Thought Fish Would Come in Handy?

By Sandy, aged 9

Fish are good,
Fish are great
The swim in the sea
We catch them with bait

Fish are good
Fish are great
They save lives
We eat them off a plate

Splish, splash, splosh
They swim through the sea,
Eating water plants and algae

Fish are great and that is why
We eat them off a plate!

Child Labour

by Miriam

Child labour, child labour, child labour !
Child labour is very bad
Child labour is hard work
Child labour can cause health problems
Dear parents and friends
Kindly stop child labour

In my childhood stage
As a girl of five years old
Forced to cook, washing big dishes
Sweeping large compounds
Ohh. Young little girl
Thin and powerless but carrying heavy stuff
Hurting and damaging soft body
Wounds and Scars all over my body
Dear parents and friends
Brothers and sisters
Stop child labour.

Stop Child Labour

By Jacquot, aged 9

I wish for you, no child labour!
I wish for you, the right to play!
I wish for you, the right to education!
I wish for you, the right to be free!
I wish for you, no really hard work!
I wish for you, no major injuries!
I wish for you, an easier life!
I wish for you, a better life!
I wish for you, a childhood to enjoy!

Play Carefully

By Benny

Play carefully
Brothers and sisters let us play carefully
Careful play is always good
Careful play is always safe
Careful play is always Healthy

On a lovely sunshine day
Playing at home with my sister
Playing with hard sharp tools
Throwing dangerous metals
This way, that way, up and down

Careful play is always good
Careful play is always safe
Accidentally I Hurt my Sister
She cried and cried louder
Shouting, asking for help
Her left leg was bleeding
In much pain and tears
She was taken to hospital
Treated carefully with love and hope
Walking back home with a smile on her face
My heart was relieved
Brothers and sisters
Careful play is always good
Careful play is always safe
Let us play carefully

Poem to Benny: Play Carefully
By Thomas, aged 9

I agree we should play carefully,
But also try to find safer things to play with like sand.
Make things out of clay,
Make toys out of sticks,
Play running races and tag.

Poem to Benny: Play Carefully
By Timmy and Chelsea

We are children
We don't always play carefully
Don't worry

I broke my cousin's collarbone
Harry broke his leg
Lucy broke her wrist
Imogen nearly broke Gracie's thumb
Adam broke his hip
Tristan nearly broke his thumb
Liam's got a scar
Jack broke his pinky
Harley fractured his toe
Jacquot dislocated his nose
Sandy broke his shoulder
Tom broke his leg
Daniel broke his hand

We are children
We don't always play carefully
Don't worry

Poem to Benny: Understanding
By Imogen, aged 11

Careful play is always good,
Careful play is always safe,
Accidentally I hurt myself falling off a climbing frame,
It's not the same but I know the pain.

I know playing with sharp tools is dangerous,
I know we should not throw heavy metal,
I understand how you worried when it happened.

I know careful play is good,
I know careful play is safe,
I know careful play is healthy,
But sometimes we have to take risks.

My Story is About My Journey From Congo to Uganda

By Eunice, aged 14

I am just a young girl,
A girl of 14 years old;
Born in the village,
Deep in Democratic republic of Congo.
My childhood has been characterized by
sorrowful moments –
Born of a father, a father never seen all my life.
Born in a country of wars, where God seems not to exist,
Where tears replace the drinking water,
Where a cluster of problems know my name,
Wishing to die but making no sense.

I am a young girl who desires to know my father,
To enjoy his love like my other friends do.
Unfortunately, I am a child of war,
Questioning my self day and night,
Was my father a soldier, a Politician, a Christian
or a thief???

Only God knows. God lift me up; help me
regain hope for a better future.
Give me strength and courage to make wonders.

Parents, Sweet Lovely Parents

By Balula

Parents, sweet lovely parents,
I miss you so much,
When ever I see your pictures,
I always cry because I miss you.

Parents, Sweet lovely parents,
You are no where to be seen alive,
But only in pictures and dreams.
My heart is hurt and so down,
My body is so weak and helpless,
I always pray to God,
To keep you safe where ever you are.
With the help of God
I gain strength and courage
To stand on my own.
And dream a difference.

Poem to Balula: **Missing Parents**
By Tristan, aged 10–11

I don't know how it feels
Not to have my parents at my side.
It must be really hard to live like that.
If you fall over,
Your parents should rush over.
What happens if you don't have your parents
To see if you're ok?

Letter to Balula: Missing Parents
By Jack, aged 10 –11

Dear Balula,

I don't know what it is like to miss your parents or to live
without your parents by your side. I hope you find them.
My friends are all hoping the same for you. I wish I could
help you find them. I wish for you a future where stuff
like this never happens.

From Jack

OXFORDSHIRE HOSPITAL SCHOOL, ENGLAND

Introduction

**Catharine Costello,
Curriculum Leader, English and Arts**

The Oxfordshire Hospital School (OHS) is an Oxfordshire County Council (OCC) maintained Hospital School based across a number of settings throughout the county of Oxfordshire. The school serves children and young people aged 4–19 who are unable to attend their home school, due to a wide range of medical and mental health needs.

In My Imagination Clouds

By Euan, aged 6

Rip
Rop
Stomp
Qop
The elephants are here,
I know –
I was in the jungle there.

Cinnamon

By Oliver, aged 15

The cinnamon reminds me of little pellets of snow drops;
Cinnamon gives me a feeling of warmth
Stepping onto a hot desert.

Orange Cake

By Oliver, aged 15

The lovely brightly coloured orange juice drizzled down
my lip as I bit into the freshly ripe tangerine,
The smell of the home baked orange cake melted in my
nostrils
and crept into the hairs of my suffocating nose which
reached like a lightning bolt that had cracked open like a
firework.

BLOEMFONTEIN, SOUTH AFRICA
Sunflower Children's Hospice

Sunflower Children's Hospice is a non-profit organisation that provides care and compassion for all children with life-threatening and life-limiting conditions. The aim of this Hospice is to keep children within their families and communities as far as possible, with relevant supervision and support.

The outer walls of the hospice are painted with sunflowers. Each sunflower bears the name of a child who has died in the care of the hospice, and every year a service of remembrance is held. Hospice children know that they will always be remembered in this way and it provides comfort for those without families.

On Bullying

By Bonolo

Picking on your size
Is not in your books,
Your cruelty is beyond that of a hyena
Hyenas hung in the face of scared ones.

You are scary
Your fist is as big as a mountain rock
Yet it is used on souls smaller than ants,
Seeing them smile makes you aggressive
Seeing them smile makes you delighted.

Your face is like an old cloth,
A cloth that has been to fights
Been scratched, cut and full of holes

Your eyes are red as blood
Burning with fire filled with anger,
Blaming the innocent for your anger and pain.

You have so much pride,
Realising anger and pain is good;
But releasing it to others is a bad idea.

You are a lonely eagle,
Preying on a small and innocent mouse.
There is no price big enough to hold your anger.

As soon as you leave your rage
The better you could be,
The friends you could have

Orphan

By Modiponse

Being an orphan is hard
It doesn't matter how old you are
There is always a place that longs for parental love.
Growing up without parents is hurtful
It is a challenge that is faced by most children
But being an orphan should not define you
Yes being an orphan makes you different
The difference is you no longer have
The love, support and guidance you used to have.
But you are still the same person you were
When your parents were still alive.
So don't let your mind deceive you
By telling that you are an orphan.
Or want to see the possibilities beyond where you are
Though the pillar of strength you were leaning on
Has fallen.
Stand up and pick up the pieces.
Be more stronger than you were before.
They miss and long for their parents.
Long for someone who will tell them that everything is
okay
Conditions and circumstances pull you down
But just console yourself with these words,
I shall overcome.

Dear Fellow Dreamers

By Tshiu

Dear Fellow dreamers,
Let your dream be big,
Bigger than the sky above

Nobody knows your ability,
Stamina, drive.

Your dreams are your car
To get you there.

So walk a step a day,
Then millimetres, centimetres, metres
And kilometres till you get reach it.
Clouds are up there
Cheering on the dreamchasers
Miracle workers
Impossible make possible.

Abuse: Dear Abuse

By Rorisang, aged 10

I want to see a world without abuse
No women with scratches
No child with scars
No man with a fist
Saying: I'll hit you woman
I want children to have a say
Someone you know
Turning against you
Taking your money
Leaving you on the street
Locking you out of your own house
Only because they have their own problems
Taking out their frustrations on you
Only because they don't know peace and harmony
They take out this frustration on you
Don't children, women have a right
To be safe and accommodated?
Their rights trampled
They fear being around monsters
Monsters known as fellow humans
Wolves in sheep's skin/clothing
Now is the time, time to be free from the chains
Chains known as abuse
Monsters need to go to jail since they deserve it
They have a tendency
Tendency of breaking your soul
Why do you do this to me?
You have killed my soul

YORKSHIRE, ENGLAND
Hawes Primary School

Hawes Primary school is in a National Park in Yorkshire, and the town of Hawes is said to be one of England's most isolated – surrounded by high fells and rippled with dry stone walls.

Introduction
by Jackson

I have a really kind and loving teacher and my favourite subject is Maths and I don't mind English. My school is the best. I like being at school with my friends so I have company and people to talk to about things. I wish there could be more Maths and if people don't want to do it they can do something else or they could do a different subject or they could have extra play depending on the votes for the subjects or extra play. There are four classes in our school, Years 1–6. There is a reception and nursery and there is one teacher and a teaching assistant in each class.

The Countryside

By Adam

In the countryside there are fields so vast,
And dry stone walls made of grey limestone,

The farm holds animals like cows and sheep,
Which roam around in the emerald fields,
With dew on the tips of the grass,

The farm will eventually be passed down to me,
In many many years,

I am lucky to live in such a place,
So many hills, such a landscape

My Name is Esme

By Esme

I'm nine and a half years old.
My family has a sister who is a really good chef,
My Dad is a really good farmer
My Mum is really good at cheering me up.
I also have chickens and sheep as pets.
The wildlife around me makes it like home,
I love the highland cows,
The beautiful red squirrels
The green slushy fields
Most of all
Seeing
A beautiful view.

Creative world

By Lucas

I sketch the world
With the trees
And the power they give.
Just think how lucky we are
To be alive in this world of joy.
We have friends to care
Homes to live in with our family.
We give air, they give air,
We are alive

By Olivia

I open my door and look around me:
The little bits of snow left over from Winter,
The new Spring lambs prancing gracefully
In the lovely Spring snowdrops.

As I turn around, I see all my friends and shout 'Hello'
The world turns round and the sun says goodbye
As we say hello to the moon.

I close my door and go to bed
And think of all the shining stars
The same ones seen by you!

The World Around Me

By Reggie

When I'm on a football pitch I love kicking a ball,
Scoring a goal is one of the best feelings in the world.
Every team wants to win

Climbing up hills and walking country lanes,
Having fun with my mates,
Playing happily.

Looking outside only sometimes seeing snow,
Sledging and building snowmen
Having a warm and reliable house.

GAZA, PALESTINE
Prep B Secondary School

We formed a partnership with Prep B Secondary School, a girls' secondary school based in Gaza City, Palestine.

The secondary school has held several Skype exchanges with The Cotswold School in Bourton on the Water.

Words from a participating pupil from Prep B Secondary School. Gaza City:

'This is our lovely dream . . . for those suffering we imagined a new world, a happy world – few worries absence of pain – this is all we have between our 15 countries: England, Syria, Bagladesh and America.

'We expressed our missing dream through the exhange of ideas and feelings. Showed them our writings' efforts.

'We exchanged workshops that aimed to achieve social justice and safety, away from pain. The idea arrested our school and we were given the opportunity as givers of joy.

We persisted, shared and created. We shall build, like a sea bird across the seasons, with the most beautiful words rising form our pure insides calling for love and peace We share the same space. . .'

Below are poems written between 2017 and 2018:

The Captain of Peace Ship
By Isra, aged 11–14

Peace came aboard a ship,
Offloaded on the pavements of sorrows
To bring back a life that was giving in to death.
It dumps her pain into the bottom of the deep seas
So that the dawn of peace breaks out through the lifeless and the alive
To uproot the darkness and raise the birdsong loud

قبطان السلام

إسراء البنا

سلامٌ على متن سفينة

يرسو على أرصفة الأحزان

فيعيد حياة تهاوت للموت

يلقي بوجعها الى قيعان بحارٍ

فيبزغ فجر السلام مخترقاً الجمادات والاحياء

ويُبيد الظلام رافعاً صوت زقزقة الحياة

The Flowers of Peace

By Saja, aged 11–14

From the rose garden in my heart
I picked the flowers of peace,
With their essence I write this letter seeking safety.
And from my balcony I send it to the moon with love,
So that the drums of hope roll in the human heart
And the stories of the dark nights become a mere past
And these times end in the coronation of peace, king of
the universes.

من حديقة ورود قلبي قطفت زهور السلام

لأكتب بعبيرها رسالة أمان

وأرسلها من شرفتي الى القمر بحنان

لُتقْرَعَ طبولُ الامل بقلب الإنسان

وتُصبح قصص الليل الأسود في زمن كان

وينتهي الزمان بتتويج السلام ملك الأكوان .

The World of Justice

by Basant, aged 1–14

We have always dreamed of living in the world of social
justice,
We have always dreamed of living with dignity,
But our dreams will never come true if we just keep
dreaming of living.

We hope and we disperse, we live through hunger and
thirst.
What has become of your dignity oh humans
Did you forget you are humans
Did you bury your dignity? Did you forget it?
Did you forget the justice?
Wake up oh humans.
We live in a poor society with no justice
Wake up and come back to your senses!

لطالما حلمنا أن نعيش في عالم العدالة الاجتماعية .

لطالما حلمنا أن نعيش تحت ظل كرامة إنسانية

لكن لن تحقق أحلامنا إذا بقينا نحلم بالعيش ,

نتفاءل ونتفرق، نجوع ونعطش .

أين كرامتك أيها الإنسان ؟ هل نسيت أنك انسان ؟

هل كرامتك تحت الارض ؟ هل نسيت كرامتك ؟

وهل نسيت عدالتكم ؟

فلتصحُ يا إنسان . مجتمع فقير، عدالة منسية،

فلتصحُ وتعود الى رشدك.

Just a Dream
by Rana, aged 11–14

I am wandering from one place to another
I am travelling from one country to another,
I am strolling around, I am enjoying a job like no other
I learn what I want to,
Smiling all the way through.
I live in my own country,
Olive trees surrounding me,
I look out of my window at the sea ,
My window has never known war.
Oh God! I woke up . . . my dream is over,
How can I get back into it?

مجرد حلم

رنا الفيومي

انتقل من مكان لآخر ..

أسافر من دولة لأخرى ..

أتنزه،أعمل في وظيفة لا مثيل لها باستمتاع ,

أتعلم ما أريده .

البسمة لا تفارق شفتاي ..

أعيش في وطني .. وأشجار الزيتون بجواري ..

أطل من نافذة غرفتي المشرفة على البحر لا تعرف معنى للحروب .

يا الهي قد صحوت من نومي ..

وانتهى حلمي، فكيف لي أن أرجع اليه ؟

Butterfly

By Rawdha Albanna, year 9

Oh dear butterfly!
If only you would help me
And offer me your beautiful wings
So I can move in every way
not worrying about the barriers
Or the fees to pay
How wonderful it is to have wings
I would fly in the sky
And taste the clouds
Touch the stars
Reach the forests and sit on the tops of mountains
Oh dear butterfly!
How wonderful it is to have wings
So I can move in every way

روضة البنا ، الصف التاسع : " الفراشة \ حق التنقل "

الفراشة

أيتها الفراشة
لو أنك تساعديني
و تقدمي لي أجنحتك الجميلة ..
حتى أتنقل في كل مكان
و لا أفتش على الحواجز
أو أدفع ثمن الذهاب ..
ما أجمل أن يكون لي جناح ..
أحلق في السماء ..
و أتذوق السحاب ..
و ألمس النجوم ..
و أذهب للغابات ..
و أجلس على قمم الجبال
أيتها الفراشة
ما أجمل أن يكون لنا جناح ..
لأنتقل حيثما أشاء ..

Poverty

By Radha Albanna, year 9

Oh the world! oh people!
Are your hearts made of ice or what?
The child is sitting on the roadside
While you enjoy the luxury of your cars
Did the ice around your hearts not melt away yet?
Nothing is left of the child but his skeleton
Reaching out for help
Die oh poverty, die
The child is about to die
From hunger and cold
Oh people!
Are your hearts made of iron? Or steel?
Did the fire not reach your hearts yet?
When would the fire start and melt the iron away
And melt the steel away
Oh people!

Ask poverty to die
Ask poverty to go away!

الفقر

أيها العالم .. أيها الناس ..

أقلبكم من جليد أم ماذا ؟

الطفل يجلس على قارعة الطريق

و أنتم تجلسون في أفخر العربات ..

ألم يذب الجليد بعد أم ماذا ..

لم يبق الا هيكل الطفل وهو

يمد يده طالبا المساعدة ..

مت أيها الفقر ..

مت أيها الفقر ..

الطفل شارف على الموت

من جوع و من برد

أيها الناس ..

أقلبكم من فولاذ ..

أم من حديد ..

ألم تشتعل النار بعد أم ماذا ؟

متى تشتعل و تصهر الفولاذ ...

متى تشتعل و تصهر الحديد ...

أيها الناس ...

اطلبوا من الفقر أن يموت

اطلبوا من الفقر الرحيل ..

BOURTON-ON-THE-WATER, ENGLAND
The Cotswold School

The Cotswold School is a secondary school situated in Bourton-on-the-Water in the heart of the Cotswolds, a designated Area of Outsanding Natural Beauty. The Cotswold School was one of the first to test the project in 2016 and *Dream a Difference* has run for three years at the school. We have always worked with Year 8 English Literature classes. Pupils are mixed genders and all aged 12–13 years. We publish here a small selection of poems from 2017/18 and from 2018/19.

Introduction
by Flavia, Savannah and Jessica

When we first heard about this, we thought the concept was quite unique and clever, it really opened our eyes to the suffering a lot of children and adults have to go through each day. A challenge we faced was expressing our sympathy for people in Palestine in poem form. However, a benefit from this was seeing how our poems could uplift their spirit, even if it was just for a day.

Something we learnt from this was how much pain people go through and how strong the people from Palestine are.

The Sound of Freedom

By Araminta

The hoofbeats thunder
Like a million proud hearts,
But there are only two.

Two ears point forwards
The trees rock past
Forever calm

Everything sways in a rocking horse movement.
Here, both horse and rider are free.
All deserve this happiness.

Light the Way Home

By Lara Metayer

This poem is written to all the children in Palestine

It seems dark and all that was yours is supposedly gone.
Its hard and life is far from serenity.
But no matter what they say
And though light may seem stamped out
There's always hope
And there's always light.
Do not go down without a fight.
When a single candle is blown out by the harsh, bitter
wind,
The beacon on the headland stays shining
Forever still shining
Lighting your way home.

Our Poem About an Eagle

**By Oscar, Frank,
Josh and Elijah**

I breathe in the sweet perfume of the mountain
As I fly down towards the river;
I gift you my wings so you can fly with me,
We can be free.

I feel the wind flowing through my feathers,
Gliding down towards the ground.
As if in a plane – we are safe,
About to land.

The Devil's Garden

By Isla

From dawn to dusk they all suffer pain
As the devil washes hope away
Covers it in disgust and a little bit of sadness,
Plus a sprinkle of pain and a touch of madness.
This is the way the devil keeps his garden

But what if we could add something to his mixture,
We could maybe bring hope back into the picture
If we add some hope and a little bit of kindness,
A sprinkle of peace and a touch of honesty
This could be the way the devil kept his garden

Hope and Memory

By Rhiannon

As the dust grains cover
Your fallen brothers
You must say this last goodbye.
Night is now falling
So ends this day,
In sorrow and toil
And your homes far away

Sleep now
And dream of those who came before
They are calling,
From across a distant shore
Go to sleep and forget
Your grief and your fear
Today ends in sadness
But tomorrow brings hope

Lay down your head
And close your sleepy eyes
And when again they open
The sun will rise
Deep in the meadow
Hidden far away
A cloak of leaves
A moonbeam ray

Forget your woes and let
Your troubles lay
And when again its morning
They'll wash away

The Bird

By Harry

There was a bird white with fear
It could not fly in the sky, oh dear.
It's colour and size
Were majestic to the eyes
If only the bird was not so white with fear.

Dusk and Dawn

By Agatha

Dusk falls as the shadows lose the outlines of the houses;
The rubble covering the ground;
The walls gone from a family home
And in that home, the last memories fade
As the owners walk to a safer place.
This is not the world that we should know,
Nor the world that should exist
But the one in the faintest nightmares
That are forgotten at dawn.

Light

By Grace

Light comes at dawn
Light comes at dusk
But dawn always takes longer to come.
These long dark days
Spent sitting, waiting
For something to happen,
But no spark appears.

I always try to follow the light
Whenever it appears
But wherever I follow it to,
It leads back to here.
Hours, days, weeks months and years
Waiting for something to happen

My father used to speak of a thing called 'hope'.
Ridiculous idea!
As if such a thing could exist here.
Although, in hours like these
Where I can actually see
The bright white moon,
Sometimes, not always, but sometimes
I can see a spark
A spark, that isn't much I know
It isn't perfect
But it's a start
A possible start of something new.

The Snowflake

By Elijah

As the sun rose over the land, ready to scorch the earth and its inhabitants, the children cried out for relief from the sweltering rays but none came.

Suddenly dark clouds shroud the skies and plunged the land into darkness. The children had no idea what to do until a single snowflake fell from the sky and then another and before they knew it, they were buried in the light white powder

And even though they knew it could not last forever, it was bliss – for now.

My Poem

By Ollie

Up in the war ridden sky
Higher than the bee does fly
There lies a glimmer of hope
Only seen by a telescope
But not invisible
Only unseen by the naked eye
Higher than the bee does fly.

*Below is a small selection of poems written in the third year of the project from an exchange conducted between **Prep B Gaza Secondary School** and **The Cotswold School** between September 2018 and January 2019.*

Introduction

by Rebecca Witts

We have been corresponding with a school in Palestine, writing poems to each other. Their poems opened our eyes to the destruction and sorrow in the world, and showed us how lucky we are to be living in the place we do. They expressed their sadness, fear but also their hope, whilst we wrote of hope, love, peace, and kindness, wishing them happiness and joy. It was an amazing experience, which taught us that even though life has its hardships, hope can still be found

It was hard to find ways to write to them of happiness and love, whilst seeing how hard their lives are, and acknowledging that joy is hard to find for them. It was lovely when we were able to skype them, and see these people we had been writing to, and who had been writing back to us. It was inspirational to see how they still had hope in their situation. We enjoyed it hugely, and are grateful for the opportunity we were given in this project.

A Whisper
By Israa

How long will you continue to drown in tears?
Arise towards the moon of the skies,
And light up the stars of hope
Sprinkle the scent of roses into the darkness
To bring back life into the blackness.

همسة

(إسراء البنا)

إلى متى ستظل تغرق بالبكاء ؟

قم نحو بدر السماء

وأشعل نجوم الآمال

انثر عبير الورد في الظلام

لتعيد الحياة إلى السواد

I Mourn for You, Israa Al Banna
By Bertie

I mourn for you who live your lives beneath the
exploding stars,
I mourn for you whose flowers are overwatered
with blood and tears,
I mourn for you who live your lives without safety of
salvation.
Someday
The dove of peace will fly to you and the rains
will rise,
The angel of life will come to you and then hope
shall be immortal
The dog of loyalty shall come to you and then
the grass will grow
And you will play in your gardens without any
worries at all.

A Whisper to Israa

By Zoe

Sprinkle the scent of roses into the darkness,
To light up the path towards love,
For the skies to open from above
To replace all tears with happiness,
Despite all that a voice grows in my heart
To spread a scent of devotion.

A whisper is all it takes,
To change a traumatised life,
With kindness.
You deserve a fearless night –
For once.

Still that voice in my heart
Sends the love you need
To you, From just
A whisper

I am 13 years old. I was born in Bristol. I have 1 sister, 1 half brother, 3 stepbrothers and 1 step sister. My favourite hobby is horseriding. I remember when I did my first ballet recital and the lights were blinding and the stage was cold and I forgot all my dances.

Voices

By Nour

I hear the sounds of destruction, of killing, of mothers'
cries

I wonder: what is the suffering for? And when will the
doors be open?

I am just a child who lost her freedom, lost her childhood

And despite all that, a voice grows in my heart, in my
mind

A voice calling: Hold on, for soon the morning will shine
and darkness will disappear

And another voice says: Soon the butterflies of freedom
will fly

And the birds will sing melodies of peace in the green
gardens

أصوات

(نور حمدان)

أسمع صوت دمار .صوت قتل صوت صراخ الأمهات

أتساءل لماذا هذا العذاب ؟ ومتى سوف تنفتح الأبواب ؟

أنا مجرد طفلة فقدت حريتها ..فقدت طفولتها

رغم ذلك صوت يكبر في عقلي في قلبي

صوتٌ ينادي اصمدي فقريباً سيشرق الصباح

ويزول الظلام

وصوت آخر يقول : قريباً ..ستطير فراشات الحرية

وتنشد العصافير أنغام السلام في الحدائق الخضراء

A Message of Hope for Nour

By James

Among the sorrows
Among the cries,
Among the missiles,
Among those mourning,
Among those who died
Hope will still be there,
Light will shine above all.

To wake in a new place,
To find a new heart,
Here there is no fear of gunfire or bombs,
A place of hope,
A place of life,
A place where war does not exist.

This has been a place of beauty,
A place of life,
Destruction has not been discovered yet,
But this Neverland has gone,
Now only fear and hatred rule,
People too scared to go outside;
One day this place will be restored,
Restored back to its beauty
Or is this just in my head
A wish that might not come true?

People will fall,
People will be remembered,
People will still have fear
And keep hope
Regain your strength,
As one day you can be the saviour
The saviour to your own kingdom.

We are made to live,
We are born to die,
But never should anyone die so early
Or be harmed in such a way,
Living in a horror film,
Scared of our own future;
So let's stand together,
Raise each other's pride
And together evil will fall

I was born 20/10/2005. My family are the people in my home. My favourite pet is a dog. I remember clearly when we Skyped Palestine. If I could make one change for the world it would be peace.

*Left &
below
right*:
Children
from the
Island
Hospice,
Zimbabwe

Above and right:
Nazmul Huda **working at
Compassionate Care Korail,
Dhaka, Bangladesh**

Above, right & below:

Writing poetry and Skype calls between years 5 and 6, Chadlington School, and Bondeko Refugee Settlement, Kampala, Uganda

Left:
The poetry exchange group from Bondeko Refugee Settlement, Uganda

Below: Prep B Secondary School, Gaza City, Palestine

Below: Between The Cotswold School and Prep B Secondary School

Right:

Poetry workshop with girls at Prep B Secondary School, Gaza City, Palestine

Above and left:

Reading at the Sierra Poetry Festival in April 2018.

Students from Grizzly Hill School Nevada, gave readings of poetry from their sessions with workshop leader, Conrad Cecil (*pictured*)

Dartington Primary
School poems

Left:

'Butterfly' by Madeleine

Below:

'My Amazing Trousers'
poem by Zach

Butterfly,
Understanding of peace,
Time travel through Love,
Travel in magic,
Enter laphter,
Runaway from the dark,
Fun and me is loyalty,
Love kindness, love to be happy,
You can have peace, just like me.

By Madeleine

my amazing trousers:

are made of bubbles and clouds

Smell like a bubble bath

Sound like a waterfall

can stop global warming

can save the sea

could stop wars

are awsome to me

Love is both genders (Pets)

pets are like best friends who always
stay by your side.
Pets are like teddies you can
cuddle whenever you want.
pets are like good luck charmes that
never leave you.
pets are like clouds that float
in the sky.
By sanchia

Right:

Poem
'Love is
Both
Genders'
by
Sanchia

v

Below & right: During the war, an artist and gallery owner challenged young people from 500 primary schools in Damascus to make an image of their 'dreams for the future'. These images were collected by Manas Ghanem, a Syrian lawyer who worked for Unicef, who sent them to UK schools to inspire their writing to young people in Syria.

Above & below:

Entered drawings by young people in Damascus.

শীত এর একটি সুন্দর ছবি দেখতে চাই সুখমা আছাই নিজে দিকে (খেলছে)।

In Korail Slum, our partner *Compassionate Care Korail* organised an art and poetry competition to reach as many as possible of the 2,000 children attending informal learning centres in the Bangladesh slum. Some of the winning entries from the art competition are printed here

Top: Winner 'My Dream World' by Rima, age 9.

Left: Entries by Marziya *& below*: by Sabbir

শীত এমনি এমন একটা সুন্দর দেশের চাই খেলব আরাই আবারাইক আবাব করব সুখে বা প্রীতিনির আরাই একবারে থাকব এবং খেলাধুলা করব

The Glistening Dawn

by Fatima

Something glimmers in the skies during the glistening
dawn,
Perhaps a shining star, perhaps a dream ascending
Come with me towards the morning sun, not the winter
clouds
And look how the stars shine freely, even when they are
covered with the clouds.

الفجر الوضّاء

(فاطمة عاور)

شيء لمع في السماء في ذلك الفجر الوضّاء

ربما نجمة تلمع وربما حلمُ صعد نحو السماء

هيّا معي نحو شمس الصبح لا غيم الشتاء

وانظر إلى تلك النجوم تلمع حُرّة مهما غطتها الغيوم

I am a Child, and I Dream

By Abla

I am a child
My doll was stained with blood
My eyes were screaming from the destruction
And my notebook was filled with ashes
This is our state; we are tortured, persecuted and killed.
I am a child and I dream
Of peace and love and abundance
I dream of playing in the garden
And not be betrayed by a black raven
I am a child and I dream
I am a touch of love, a jasmine, a poet of adoration
I am a caring soul born amidst the destruction and
dreams of freedom
That is me, a child, and I dream

أنا طفلة...وأحلم

(عبلة جابر)

أنا طفلة

لعبتي تلوثت بالدماء

وصاحت عيناي من الدمار

ودفتري امتلأ بالرماد

هذا حالنا نُعذّب و نُؤسر ونُقتل

أنا طفلة .. وأحلم

بالسلام والحب والرفاهية

أحلم بأن أجلس في الحديقة وألعب

ولا يغدر بي غراب أسود

أنا طفلة .وأحلم

أنا لمسة من الحب

أنا ياسمينة وأنا شاعرة العشق

أنا حنونة نبتت وسط الدمار وحلم الحرية
هذه أنا

طفلة وأحلم

'Wait, Abla!' For Abla

By Jasmine

I am a child,
And I pray for love and peace
For the miracle of a loving world,
A world with an united army,
A world with a caring family.
Yet my prayers are unanswered,
Death and destruction,
Power and prejudice remain,
Where children cry out for light,
Hidden in the dark.
But I assure you there is hope,
Amidst the fog and the ashes,
Waiting, waiting, waiting.
You are tortured, persecuted and killed,
While others are praised, fed and cared for.
I assure you the flower will bloom,
The flower of hope and peace,
Wait Abla, as I will wait with you,
For peace and love and serenity,
In this bitter and torn world,
Wait, Abla, just hold on,
To the minuscule thread of hope
That barely holds this world together
My had reaching for yours:
We feel beautiful powerful and privileged
But we are broken weak and afraid.
Wait, Abla
Just wait.

*My name is Jasmine and I am 13 years old. I was born in
London but now live in the Cotswolds, a really beautiful place*

with endless fields, rows of flowers and trees. I love art and sport. If I could change one thing about myself I would make my knees healthier so that they are not always covered in bandages from injuries and so I can run more.

The Love of Life

by Batoul

Our future is filled with fog
Smelling of blood
Our present is a flower with torn petals
But it continues to defy death
And spread its scent all around
We are suffocating but we are still alive
Because we loved life despite the hard times.

حُبّ الحياة

(بتول السكافي)

مستقبلنا يكسوه الضباب

وتفوح منه رائحة الدماء

حاضرنا زهرة تمزّقت أوراقها

لكنها مازالت تتحدّى الموت

وتنشر عبيرها في الأرجاء

نحن نختنق لكنّنا مازلنا على قيد الحياة

لأنّنا أحببنا الحياة

رغم قساوة الأيام

'Beyond the Bitter Fog', for Batoul

By Eve

Beyond the bitter fog,
There's a beautiful place,
Somewhere to feel safe and joyful,
Your won peaceful space.

Beyond the bitter fog,
There's emerald green fields
Where flowers replace dead bodies
A place armed with shields.

Beyond the bitter fog,
The smell of blood has gone
In its place are fragrant flowers
Hiding the problems
That we must act upon.

A More Beautiful Human, a Poem to Eve

By Batoul

I asked life: Are you getting uglier every day?
It answered: if you cannot see the bright side, that doesn't
deny its existence
So it's better to see things from a different perspective
For when you see fate more beautiful
And you see differences as perfection
And learn determination from the waves, pride from the
mountains, and softness from the flowers,
Then you will be another human, a more beautiful
human.

إنسان أجمل

(بتول السكافي)

سألت الحياة أأنت تزدادين قبحاً يوماً بعد يوم

فأجابت إن لم تكن ترى الجانب المشرق فهذا لا ينفي وجوده

لذا فمن الأفضل أن ترى الأشياء من منظور آخر

فلترَ الأقدار جمالاً

ولترَ الاختلاف كمالاً

ولتأخذ من أمواج البحر عزيمتها وإصرارها

ومن الجبال شموخها

ومن الأزهار رقتها

عندها ستكون إنساناً آخر

إنساناً أجمل

I Will Ascend

by Rawdha

I will ascend to the top despite all the attempts to crush
my will
I will ascend to fulfil my dream
To achieve everything beautiful
I will be the change
And I will be the key that opens rusty locks of life
Yes, I will ascend

سأصعد

(روضة البنا)

سأصعد للقمم رغم كل محاولات إحباط عزيمتي

سأصعد لأحقق حلمي

لأحقق شيئ جميل

سأكون أنا التغيير

وأنا المفتاح الذي يفتح أقفال الحياة المتأكسدة

نعم سأصعد

My Dreams Are Like a Bubble

By Israa

Here are my dreams, I look at them
How perfectly beautiful they are
Although they are entrapped from all directions
And every time I strengthen them they become more
vibrant with rainbow colours
I imagine them a bubble
I support it and I blow into it
It grows bigger, and becomes more vibrant with rainbow
colours
And it starts moving and moving
Until it touches the intended spot and explodes
To spread its mist and revive the dead hopes

أحلامي كالفقاعات

(إسراء البنا)

هاهي أحلامي .أنظر إليها

كم أنها جميلة في غاية الإتقان

مع أنها محاصرة من جميع الجهات

إلّا أني كلما دعمتها تزداد جمالاً بألوان الطيف

أتخيلها فُقّاعة

أدعمها وأنفث فيها

تزداد حجماً وتزداد جمالاً بألوان الطيف

وتبدأ بالمسير .. والمسير

حتى تلامس المكان المبتغى ..وتنفجر

فتنشر رذاذها   ..لتحيي الآمال الميتة

A New World

By Lorna

I see your hands
Stretching, reaching for a life where you no longer need
hope;
A life where you don't know worry,
Where butterflies represent peace not hope for peace.
A butterfly, wings spread wide and open
Welcomes newcomers to this new world
Away from the forgotten violence and pain.
I will create a world where you don't have to surrender to
reality
But instead embrace peace.
Peace is a bubble of silence and happiness
And if you're not careful it can be broken
With a single act of terror.
Together we will work to make the bubble bigger,
Sturdier and permanent.
People from far and wide will write together to fight the
terror
And build a wall to separate the traumatising past
From this glorious future.

To Failure

By Israa

A good night to you,
For now, it is time for life to return to its dreamers.
We will not fall from the mountaintops into the valleys.
We will connect our hopes and deter our pains.
We will wipe away the tears rushing from its quarries,
and we will soar into the sky.
Farewell to you oh failure, we will bring back the
euphoria of success.
We will over come the pitfalls of the times.

أيها الفشل
إسراء البنا

نوماً هنيئاً لكَ

لقد آن الأوان كي تعود الحياة إلى حالميها

لن نسقط من قمم الجبال إلى دركها

سنربط أوصال آمالنا ونردع آلامنا

سنمسح العبرات المتفجرة من محاجرها

وسننطلق نحو عنان السماء

أيها الفشل وداعاً لك فسوف نعيد نشوة النجاح

وسنتغلب على عثرات الزمان

A Poem in Response to Israa.

By Olivia

The sea of tears will drain away,
People will rejoice to see their family,
Stars will be littered with hope and joy,
Cries no longer fill the air;
The darkness will clear and life will grow;
Colour will fill the streets with plants;
Laughter is the only sound,
This is the land.

Waves crashed,
Now they are calm;
The dark sea is now a clear blue;
People are swimming, splashes fly through the air,
Fish are brushing past your feet;
No large metal boats take up the sea;
The summer sun will reflect in your eyes
This is the sea.

The sky is blue and dotted with clouds,
The squawks of birds echo,
No planes or helicopters ruin the day.
At night the sunset is bright red
In the morning a playful pink,
This is the sky.

Contradictions of a Painting

By Batoul

Gaza is the strangest painting ever
Love and War have met in it
And Pain and Hope have met with a strange attraction
In it, great dreams meet with short days in perfect harmony
And blood merges with the colour of roses
Its sky is grey, adorned with bullets
High rising buildings next to rubbles of Ash and Stones
Next to it, the children with messy hair, dusty skin and dusty clothes would sit
Painting the bright dream of tomorrow
Their hearts silently playing the national anthem.

(تناقضات لوحة)

غزة أغرب لوحة على الإطلاق .
فقد التقى فيها الحب والحرب
واجتمع فيها الألم والأمل بتجاذب غريب
وتجتمع فيها الأحلام الكبيرة مع الأيام القصيرة بكل تناسق .
وتندمج فيها الدماء مع لون الزهور .
سماؤها رمادية مزينة بطلقات الرصاص .
مع حمام يحمل أغصان الزيتون .
عمارات شاهقة بجوار كومات رمادٍ وحجارة .
يجلس عندها أطفال مشعثي الشعر ،
مغبري البشرة والملابس .
يرسمون حلم الغد المشرق .
وتعزف قلوبهم نشيد الوطن بصمت .

(بتول السكافي)

Be Like Them

by Rana

Hopes that have been built by people who removed the impossible from their minds.

They are certain that they will overcome all difficulties.

They have lived the bitterness and cruelty of days and they didn't not pay attention to the obstacle on the road.

They continued their journey on their path with confidence and excellence.

And turned their hopes from a dream into reality

How beautiful is optimism, and how great are optimists.

Yes, Be like them.

(كن مثلهم)

آمال قد شيدت بأيدي أناس نزعوا المستحيل من أذهانهم .

هم على يقين بأن سيجتازون كل الصعاب .

عاشوا مرارة الأيام وقسوتها ولم يلتفتوا لعثرات الطريق .

واصلوا مسيرهم نحو دربهم بكل ثقة وإتقان .

حوّلوا أمانيهم من حلم إلى واقع .

ما أجمل التفاؤل .. وما أعظم المتفائلين ..

نعم ... كن مثلهم .

(رنا الفيومي)

The Hunter of Dreams

By Mais

I will work as a hunter in my dreams
In the hope that I will find the fish that swallowed my
dream
In the hope that the sea would sooth my pains
In the hope that waves would gift me pearls of love and
seashells of hope.
I am still searching, withstanding, praying
I believe in peace
I wait for a ray of light and love

صياد الأحلام

(ميس الريم الفيومي)

سأعمل صياداً في أحلامي.

عساني أجد تلك السمكة التي ابتلعت حلمي.

عساه البحر يخفف أوجاعي.

عساها الأمواج تهديني لآلئ حب ومحارة أمنيات.

ما زلت أبحث .. أصمد.. أصلي..

أؤمن بالسلام..

أنتظر شعاع النور والحب..

والسعادة .. وأجمل الأحلام

The Hunter

By James

We have been turned inside out,
Our dreams have been hunted
And are now trapped inside our own bodies.
They scream to be released, set free,
But our cornered by the hunters,
The end is near.
Now look at us,
All you can hear is the sound of our crying.

The Hunter

Collective poem from Year 8, the Cotswold School

The hunter standing in the wood,
His sights aimed at the deer,
Trigger at the ready,
His arm strong, his finger steady,
The sun shines through, its prayers answered,
Giving the deer the chance to leave.
Don't let your dreams escape, just believe.

For All the Children in Palestine

By Maite

They did say,
Wait for a few days and the light will come,
But the days and years you waited,
Have still not led to light.

You are the ones that can break the chains
Preserving the happiness you have in your hearts and
lives.
Change the monsters that imprisoned you
And make them your angels

My name is Maite and I am 12 years old. I was born in Oxford.
I remember when my mother told me I had a sister but she never
made it to see the world around her or to feel the sun.
My favourite thing to do is play hockey because it clears my
mind of all my worries.

The Rifle's Bullets

Collective poem from Year 8, the Cotswold School

The devious bullets lay dead on the ground,
Beaten at their own game.
The ghostly souls of the elderly,
Women and children roam freely,
Like flowers they grow from the fallen bullets of war.
Maybe peace is only a dream –
You will only find it
If you keep on writing.

Brief Biographies of Palestinian Poets

Nour

I am Nour. I was born on 30/06/2005. My family is
of two brothers, myself and my mother and father.
I prefer the life of adventure and to live with my
family.

If I could do something for the world, it would be to
spread love and joy between people.

Fatma

I was born in Tolkarm on 11/6/2004. I live in a
family of two brothers, two sisters and my parents. I
now live in Gaza. I remember the happiness and fun
of my childhood and the stories of my grandmother.

I prefer the life of adventure. I like to be alone to
think and meditate. As for the world, I wish that all
the homeless children in the world would have
education in schools for free and I wish the best for

Abla

My name is Abla. I was born on 24/05/2004 from the Jaber family.

I have a family of a father, a mother, three brothers and one twin sister.

My nationality is Palestinian from Gaza. War steals my loved ones and my time, but my ambition is bigger than it and my dreams are as wide as the sea.

I like poetry and writing stories. I aspire to be a famous writer and poet and journalist reporter.

A lot of children have dreams but the absence of peace makes it hard to accomplish.

Rawdha

I am Rawdha. I was born in Gaza, Palestine; the best place in the universe as it is the source of my strength and perseverance.

I have two brothers and three sisters. I have a lot of dreams that save me from some of the darkness. My favourite hobby is to write.

Nesma

My name is Nesma and I was born on 16/01/2004. I am from Palestine and was born in Gaza.

I love life and always aspire to achieve my dreams and ambitions, I love to plant happiness in the hearts of everyone around me.

My favourite hobbies are reading and writing and I always look for the good. If I could give happiness and love to the world I would do that by plucking the roots of hatred and planting the seeds of love among people.

Saja Abdou

My name is Saja and I am happy to be able to introduce myself to you.

I was born in Gaza on 19/05/2003. I am Palestinian and this is the greatest honour life has given me. I have one sister and three brothers, I am the eldest.

Our house is in the city centre. My childhood was filled with destruction and war, but I didn't succumb to it, but rather coloured it with bright colours.

Mais

My name is Mais. I was born in Jordan on
16/06/2003.

I have four brothers younger that me. I moved to my
home country when I was five

I entered my country along with the sounds of
missiles and assaults.

My ambition is stronger than war and my dreams
are wider than space

I have several hobbies like writing poetry, thoughts
and stories. I am doing my best to be a doctor in the
future.

DAMASCUS, SYRIA
Al Farah Choir of Joy

We formed a partnership with the *Al Farah Choir of Joy* from Damascus, Syria; a group which was created and led for 20 years in Damascus by Father Elias Zahlawi, father of Our Lady of Damascus Church. Children in the choir aged 9–15, wrote to children in America and in Buckinghamshire and shared their experiences over several Skype exchanges.

We are Girls

**Written in a Skype exchange with the UK,
January 2019**

We are girls,
We are strong,
We keep walking ahead.
Sometimes we falter,
Sometimes we fall,
Then we get up
Stronger than before.
We ignore the war,
We stay together.
We learn strength from each other.
Bombs fall on our houses,
Shells smash the balconies,
Shatter the windows.
Still we stay strong
Still we wait
Our weapons are stronger than theirs:
Love and Patience,
Determination to see the day
When war will end
And Peace return.

My Dear Grandfather

by Miryam, aged 13

Once upon a time, in a calm day, angels came and took
you from me.
You went up there, and you are protecting me.
You became my guardian angel,
You will never be forgotten, it is impossible.
As long as I am alive, you will live in my mind.
I will carry you with me and hide you in my heart.
Your light will continue to shine and never fade.

You didn't tell me you were leaving,
You didn't say goodbye .
You left before I knew.
A hundred times I wished you were beside me,
A hundred times I cried.
I loved you when you were alive,
I will continue to love you when you are dead.
No one can fill up your place in my heart,
Only you can stay there.

I wish you knew how much I love you,
I wish I had the time to tell you what you mean to me,
Your place is still empty and no one would take it.
Your chair in the kitchen,
Your bed,
Your sofa in the living room.

I still remember the sound of your wooden slippers,
And how I can hear the sound of your keys in the door.
I remember how loud the TV always is,
And how you woke up in the summer to eat watermelons.
I remember we once went to buy fruits and you kept me
by your side.
We bought manga and coconut and cream,
You trusted me. I was your Miryam you loved so much,
My dear grandpa.

I love you so much,
And when I come up to you, you will be waiting for me by the door,
And you will say Welcome! Give me a kiss! And I will give you a hundred .
I cannot stop writing but I must.
Rest in peace grandpa,
I love you.
This is not a farewell, but a goodbye till we meet again.

Your beloved granddaughter
Miryam

كان يا مكان في قديم الزمان، بيوم هادي، اجوا الملايكة وأخذوك مني...
صرت أنت فوق قاعد، وعم تحميني، صرت أنت ملاكي الحارس.
أنت ما تنتسى هاد شي مستحيل
طال ما أنا عايشة أنت لح تضل بفكري لح احملك معي و خبيك بقلبي ضوك،
لح يضل عم يشع بعمرو ما لح ينطفي

أنت ما قلتلي رايح أنت
ما قلتي باي
أنت رحت قبل ما اعرف
ميت مرة تمنيتك جنبي و ميت مرة بكيت
كنت حبك كتير و هلق أ لح ضل حبك أكيد
بقلبي ألك محل ما حدا بعبي وحدك أنت بتقعد فيه
..ياريتك لو تعرف قديش بحبك
ياريتني لحقت قلك أنا أنت شو بالنسبة ألي
محلك لسا فاضي و محدا بياخدو ابدا
كرسيك بالمطبخ و تختك و كنباية غرفة القعدة
لهلئ بتذكر صوت شحاتك الخشب

وكيف صوت مفتاحك عم يفتح الباب
لهلئ بتذكر كيف تلفزيونك كان دايما عالي
وكيف بالصيف بتفيق بليل بتاكول بطيخ
بتذكر مرة رحنا سوا شترينا فواكي قعدت جنبك و وقتها شترينا منغا و جوز هند و قشطة
ثقتك فيني كانت كتير كبيرة ة أنو أنا مريومة قلبك لبتحبا كتير
جدو حبيبي بحبك بحبك كتير
بس إجي لعندك لفوق بدك تكون ناطرني عالباب وبدك تقلي اهلا و سلوة و بدك تقلي ما عطييني بوسة بس لح كون عطيتك مية
مع أني ما عم اقدر وقف كتابة بس حاجة
الله يرحمك جدي
بحبك كتير
هذا ليس الوداع بل إلي اللقاء

حفيدتك مريم

It is Said

by Miryam, aged 13

Truths are disappointing sometimes,
Everything is limitless in dreams, everyone is perfect,
love is eternal and happiness is forever.

Our childhood stories tell us a lot of beautiful tales,
They also tell us about all the fears
that we will live in the future one after the other.

The stories tell that fraudsters stole your belongings and
money,
and that spoiled princesses do not like the world they are
born into.

Where am I in this story?
Am I a sleeping princess waking up after a hundred years
with a kiss?
Or a bad queen?

Am I a girl who lost her shoe? Or an evil witch?

Who am I?

I do not care who I am in these stories
Because I will make myself a hero in my own story,
and it will be told for generations to come.

يُحكى

هي الحقائق مخيبة الأمل أحيانا

كل شيء غير محدود في الأحلام، الجميع مثالي

الحب أبدي، السعادة دائمة

حكاياتنا الطفولية تروي لنا الكثير من القصص الجميلة

ولكنها تروي أيضا لنا عن كل تلك المخاوف، التي سنعيشها في المستقبل واحدة تلو الأخرة

الحكايات تحكي أن المحتالين سلبوا منك أملاكك وأموالك، وأن الأميرات المدللات لا يعجبهم العالم الحالي الذي خلقوا فيه

أين أنا في هذه الحكاية إذا؟

هل أنا أميرة تستيقظ من نومها بقبلة بعد مئة سنة؟ أم ملكة سيئة؟

هل أنا فتاة أضاعت حذائها؟ أم ساحرة شريرة؟

من أنا؟

لا يهمني من أنا في هذه القصص لأنني سأصنع من نفسي بطلة قصتي الخاصة، و سيحكى فيها لأجيال و أجيال

NEVADA COUNTY, CALIFORNIA, USA

Grizzy Hill School to Choir of Joy, Syria *'International Exchange' poems*

When we think of international exchange, we think of exchanging currency. In the poems **'International Exchange'** *we explored what it would be like to exchange senses, considering what we could trade, and what we could actually experience together.*

International Exchange
Amrita, aged 11, Grizzly Hill

If I send you the scent of my forest, fresh and clear rain
still on the branches,
Will you send me your hope?

If you send me the sound of sirens,
I will send you the sound of the cold evening wind.

If I you could feel the soft bark of the manzanita tree,
could I feel the warm sand where you are?

Together, we see the same moon,
us in the freezing early morning
and you in the warm, dark night.

International Exchange

Rosemary, aged 8, Grizzly Hill

If I send you the smell of a wet, mossy oak tree
will you send me a rainy day, and a crocus popping out of
the grass?

If you send me the sound of a blue bird singing a new
song
I will send you one million sad California poppies
opening.

If I send you the taste of fresh snow
will you send me the taste of rain dripping off of stone
walls?

Together, we see the same stars in a black sky.

International Exchange
Annika, aged 10, Grizzly Hill

If I send you the smell of a freshly picked orange lily
will you send me sand from a desert near you?

If you send me the sound of windstorms in the middle of
summer
I will send you the sound of hungry Blue Jay chicks
chirping for food.

If I send you the taste of ripe blueberries
will you send me a lemon to squeeze in my tea?

If you could feel my dog's thick fur
could I feel all of the hard wind that the war blows over
you?

Together we see the same stars in the sky.

'**Looking at Your Language**' is *a poem based on a discussion with students after looking at a handout of the Arabic alphabet, and an unranslated poem, written in Arabic. Their interpretations of the shapes and lines reminded them of lead to their reactions.*

Looking at Your Language
Patti, 7th grade, Grizzly Hill

The shapes of your letters remind me of vines swaying in the wind

Your words look like scribbles of beauty

If I could translate, I think you might be saying how lovely the world is

I would love to say to you, how rare and elegant your words are.

Looking at Your Language
Joan, 4th Grade, Grizzly Hill

The shapes of your language's letters remind me of music notes
floating on the air

Your words look like a woodchuck tail patting a wide log

If I could translate, I think you might be saying, 'Hi, my name is . . . '

I would love to say to you, in my language, 'I love pizza.'

Looking at Your Language
Tavia, 7th grade, Grizzly Hill

The shapes of your language's letters remind me of the swirls
and shapes of music, and even though nothing plays,
I can still hear it.

Your words look like jewelry that shines, shaped like spiral diamonds.

If I could translate, I think you might be saying 'Thank you.'

I would love to say to you in my language, 'I wish the violence and war

was over, I hope the pain will go away and will not come again'.

Looking at Your Language
Virginia, 4th grade, Grizzly Hill

The shapes of your language's letters remind me of a
green oak,
swaying in the wind.

Your words look like budding maple leaves.

If I could translate, I think you might be saying, 'I want
you to be my friend.'

I would love to say to you, in my language, 'I hope you
will be my friend'.

NEVADA COUNTY, CALIFORNIA, USA
Washington Ridge School

Introduction

By Conrad Cecil

In Eastern Nevada County (Northern California), in the Tahoe National Forest, in the Little Town of Washington (population 120), is a 1900s one-room schoolhouse where six students aged between 8 and 14 form one of the smallest schools in the United States. The bell on top of the building is rung by hand every morning to start the day: that bell also serves as an alarm for the town in case of fire or flood. Esther Pearcy, herself a mother of two young children, and Julie, the teaching assistant, together run the school: preparing and dispensing lessons in all subjects, cooking and serving breakfast and lunch, organizing field trips, educating the students and being there for their crises, and managing their energy.

Washington is at the bottom of a canyon in the Sierra Nevada mountain range, where the South Fork of the Yuba River roars through. For months of the year, snow stands six feet high all around. In Spring, the river is swollen with snowmelt water, pure and crystalline. The steep canyon is thickly wooded with pine trees, up to the ridge, miles above. Nobody passes through Washington. The original residents came to find gold in the 19th century, and today's residents live in remoteness and isolation.

I came to Washington School to teach the children to write poetry about their world, and to share that poetry with children in Damascus, Syria, members of 'the Choir of Joy'. Esther and I worked together over several weeks in March and April 2019, introducing the children to poems and poetry, and to the history and culture of Syria. We looked at poems by Emily Dickinson, Blake, and A. A. Milne, and we began to write our own poems together, about the world we live in, or about worlds we dream about. The result was six very different poems, by turns fantastical, deeply personal, and then full of natural observation. The Skype session with the children in Damascus was just a beginning: an arousing of curiosity. Some of the Californian children want to become pen-pals with the Syrian children.

The Knight of Helmswood

By Mariah, 6th grade

Bright red eyes glared from beneath the trees,
At a knightsman who drank and lost his keys ,
The taste of iron danced in the air,
Our knightsman took it as a dare ,
He flung around to which he saw
An animal to be about ten feet tall!
The knight laughed, not scared in the least!
The creature lunged, ready to feast ,
His sword cut at its side ,
A battle where dagger and tooth collide ,
Claws that pierce stone ,
A mouth that breathes fire ,
Wings that charge the skies

Vampire Cats

By Lydia, 3rd grade

I feel a shiver down my spine
I cautiously creep over sticks and fallen logs
Like a caterpillar I can hear the wolf stalking me like a cat
I scamper up a tree to hide.

Parenting

By Emery, 8th grade

When you are parenting
You are just like a gardener,
Nurturing the seeds that you sow.
As a parent, you get to see and
Help your newborn children grow.
You hold their tender bodies,
Wrapping them tightly in your arms,
Day by day, year by year, they
Grow a bit more. As time passes
You may feel that they are
Drifting away, but when you
Least expect it, they envelop you in
Their arms, and gratitude fills.
The air.

My Peculiar Poem
By Noah, 5th grade

Inside the castle, and inside the king
There was an apple that was thaumaturgic
It was presumptively presentable, and
Seasonably securable, it was like a
Pear, and could smell a bee.
It magically fazapped the lung of the king
In revenge of eating him whole
And the king died
And I saw him in his throne
He was a dead goat
As far as I was concerned.

Going to Arctic Mine
By Davyn, 5th grade

Arctic mine gives me a scary feeling
A long, bumpy drive to Golden Quartz
Turn down into the forest
Park at two cement blocks
Left from an 1800s bridge
Walk across rotten planks
And walk, and walk, and walk
Abandoned cabins filled
With animals and insects
That sound like a car on a far off road.

Sister

By Andre, 3rd grade

She was 6 years old when I was born
She tells me what's right and what's wrong.
She is like a spider spinning a web
I am caught in her control.
She sometimes takes a break,
And tells me to keep working
She has freedom like a bird soaring
While I am stuck like a baby robin
Stuck being hunted by a hawk
And even though she sometimes
She does these things I still love
My sister.

LONDON, ENGLAND
Charter School, North Dulwich

Introduction

Francesca Beard, poet

London-based poet Francesca Beard worked with creative writing group *Storyverse* and librarian Jane Watkins, as well as the Year 9 English nurture group and teacher Laura Bradley at The Charter School in North Dulwich from January–March 2019.

They were to share laughter, friendship and poems with Loice Majongwe and her group of brilliant young poets from Prince Edward School in Harare. The Skype connections were sometimes glitchy, the bond of empathy and mutual respect created was strong and certain – we sincerely hope to continue this joyous, inspiring collaboration with Lucinda Jarrett and *Dream a Difference*.

Praise Poem for the Young Princes of Harare
Sent after Cyclone Idai

When I am scared
The rain pours as the pitch black spreads its ink on the
sky,
And the moon itself shines blood crimson.

You are the sun that shines in the darkness.

The rain will calm down.

You are the light that lies in the dark.

The rain will calm down,
The fog will clear away.

You are a star that brights up in darkness.

The rain will calm down
The storm will pass.

You are the praise in the song we sing to the sky.
You are the rainbow shining in the pot of gold,
You are the spirit that leads my heart.

*Lines contributed by everyone in Ms Bradley's Year 9 Nurture
Group.*

I Am

I am fish in my own tank.
I am a shark with no teeth.
I am sea without water.
I am human without bones.
I am hero to my dream.
I am a stress that can't be cured.
I am brain without ideas.
I am a leader with with no words.
I am a teacher to my world.

Daniel was born in Jamaica. His family likes to play football, his mum's cooking is delicious, especially super nice chicken and rice. If he could change one thing for his world, it would be to stop knife crime.

Time

The world is such a busy place,
Where tower blocks meet tower blocks,
Where roads meet roads,
Where the world won't stop,
Not for me not for you,
Though I wish it did too,
I wish the world could freeze,
So commuters could think,
So readers could read,
So dreamers so dream,
Just for a second . . .

Mia is from Dulwich, Sri Lanka, Brixton and Hull. She loves Leo (DC), her grandpa, Miso the cat, her parents, her life . . . She loves a lot of things. She loves you.

Sea Change

A woman throws her coat on the sofa,
A penny rolling out the pocket,
Falling into the bowls of the cracks.
She thrusts her mistake-ridden work on the sofa,
She hides many tearful days under the patchwork
pillows,
But proudly displays the happy moments,
A lost shoelace winds its way into the abyss,
Carving out tunnels,
For the warm breeze to ruffle,
At the edge of an ocean buried deep within the sofa,

A secret ocean full of lost wishes and long forgotten
dreams.

*Eva's dad is a doctor who keeps accumulating cats from
patients who can't look after them any more. One of them likes
to hold onto Eva's socks as she walks from room to room, in her
home in South London.*

I Do and I Don't

I don't have a dad. But I do have a mum.
I don't have a brother. But I have a sister.
I don't have a dog. But I do have a cat.
I don't have a hamster. But I do have a bug.
I don't have an orange. But I have an apple.
I don't have any chocolate. But I have a sandwich.
I don't have my own room. But I do have my own house.
I don't have a key. But I have a keyring.
I don't have a million pounds. But I do have about £60.
I don't have a computer. But I have a phone.
I don't have a boyfriend.
I don't have a girlfriend. But I have friends.
I don't have any tears left to cry. But I do have emotions
to express.
I don't have any tights. But I have a mountain of socks.
I don't have much patience. But I only have one lesson
left.
I don't have an acting agent. But I do have a good school.
I don't have brown eyes. My eyes are grey.

*There's quite a lot of information about Zarah in the poem
above, though not that she saw 'Girl from the North Country'
at the Old Vic four times during its short run.*

Listen

In my daisy chain I place:
a scattering of marbles
an assortment of chocolates
10 three year-olds in an orderly line
a wooden beach ball
a panda with an extra toe
a black umbrella in a sea of colour
the Philippine islands fading to grey
and two synchronised swimmers,
breaths steady and perfectly   in   sync.

*Lola Choo Antopolski loves reading, dancing (not ballet) and
football. She recently swapped Kung Fu for boxing. If she was a
character in the MCU, it would be Iron Man. If she was a
character in Brooklyn 99, it would be a mix of Jake and Amy.*

I am a light that goes on and off.

I am the King of eating chicken.

I am a cool-aid to diabetes.

I am TJ Kamara

I am the tan of fantastic.

I am the flash in flash.

*TJ was born on July the 8th. His family is full of nice people.
Home is the best place ever. If he could change one thing about
the world, it would be to stop terrorism.*

The Umbrella

The umbrella, the girl loved it.

Underneath the umbrella,

She put her best friend,

Her crush,

Her memories and her phone.

But outside of the umbrella,

She put her enemies,

Her ex, her embarrassing moments

And her homework.

She did this so the rain could drench things she hated on top of the umbrella,

But the things she loved would be shielded from the rain underneath the umbrella.

Naomi is a fantastic runner, she's the fastest 200 metre runner in Southwark. She likes Art and is going to study it for GCSE. Her favourite authors are Angie Thomas and Malorie Blackman.

Small Talk

Silver slick pen nib hovers on the page,
I've gotta write something, we've gotta engage,
I want to be friends but the words won't come,
I'm writing down lyrics of some half-forgotten song,
'How're you? How's life? Do you want to hang out?'
It's not a conversation, words still pour out my mouth,
Niceties, polities, empty words of nothing,
Each word that I type's another nail in my coffin,
Coffin of words, unseen people and places,
I'm talking to you but I can't see your faces . . .

Emily is in Year 9 and lives in London. She is the girl with pen on her fingers. She looks sunny but needs more sleep. (But the internet.) Dogs often prefer her over others.

I'm the Doctor to My Who

I'm the Bonjour to my Hello
I'm the Future to futuristic
I'm the Gmail to @
I am my life, my studies, my GCSEs.
I am my family, my Future,
My A-levels, my Options,
My Games, my priorities
My well-being my friends.
I am the paint to the wall
I am the window to the sun
I am the wizard to harry potter
I am the book that everybody reads.
I am a child but an adult.
I am Suleiman.

Suleiman is from Somalia, he's proud to be from Africa.

In the Bag

I'm going to throw in chicken,
Jerk chicken,
Morleys chips and burger sauce.
I'm going to throw in jollof rice
And rice and peas.
I'm throwing in football and basketball.
I'm throwing in Fortnite and Black Ops 3,
I'm throwing in my console.
I'm throwing in a shower every day.
I'm throwing in a detention this week.
I'm throwing in anyone who's ever been in a fight.
I'm throwing in that weird book I read.
I'm throwing in any one who's had a crush.

Emmanuel has seven siblings, his favourite game is Fortnite, he loves to eat chicken and he cares about the environment and his family.

Conversation

Self confidence
Noise
Muted languages that are sounds not words
But I am here now; I am where I want to be
For now
In life
See why I, why do I stand here right now?
I don't understand what they say always.
Out of context but seeing the silent noise
Being deaf to the world isn't always that,
Easy
How to connect?
To be honest I'm overthinking fifty decibels

But It's Still A Lot Of Silent Noise

*I could have another name and it wouldn't make a difference.
Still, it's Kai. I am often late and generally disorganised. I
mean, why is being organised such a big deal? If I could change
one thing, it would be my lack of self-confidence, like a second
mind that always interrupts my thoughts. I'm also a pessimist,
as you can probably tell by now.*

HARARE, ZIMBABWE
Prince Edward Secondary School

Prince Edward Secondary School, Harare, is a boys school based in the capital of Zimbabwe, Africa. The workshops have been led by the English Literature teacher, Loice Majongwe.

Hope
by Sean

A million beams
of gentle light streams,
A written hymn of
gladness joy they sing,
A joyful King of life and
not strife, give praise!
Hope dwells in every little thing,
just look around and see.
The belief of a five year old
lad in fairies and
mermaids and all things
magical and mad
 is innocence that fuels
the hearts of even the
grumpy of old
farmers to grow a mile
of a smile and do the jig
with his pig,

Just look over yonder
there and you'll see.

Once upon a time, a
huntress who knew
no care and her very
being unfair found
her hope in the most adorable of antelope,

A thousand years later,
A mother put her daughter to bed,tucked
her in and cuddled her
head,told a story of how
even a huntress could
find love in her prey.

Tales to spin and care
to share,
Let not this be
a nightmare but a glimmer of hope.

If you squint your eyes and look hard enough
you just might see!

*My name is Sean and as a poet I see the world in a whole new
way. Where others see a sunset, I see a story and by feeling,
analysis and above all belief, I begin to write!*

Rainbow

By Jared

Rainbow
Take it slow
After the rain
Pain
Massive destruction
Comes the rainbow

The hero

When, everyone feels like a zero
Save the day
Make everyone feel okay
Stay quiet during the thunderstorm
Stay true don't conform
Because when they need freedom

You will transform
To the hero

Be like a rainbow show your true colours

Be who you are
Show them that you are bizarre
And you can shine because you're a star

Show them the pain

From the rain
Was all worthwhile
To wait for the rainbow

No see them smile
Show them your style
Go the extra mile

Because you are a rainbow

By Munyaradzi

As the day gives way to the night,
Born are the fears we dread,
The ones that tie us like shoelaces and wrap us
round like rhymes,
The owls hoot their complaints
The wind hisses it's breezes and slowly
the night festers on.
I am a child of the day but as I stand now,
I have been adopted into the night time,
The peace and quiet I once longed for are rather
threatening
The visions I dream are turned violent.
In this sordid place where right is left
and left is right
I have but one option.
That is to find the light
Because the darkness which surrounds us
has become redundant.

My name is Munyaradzi and I write to try find the meaning of this world and why some things occur. I have been unsuccessful so far.

African Mother

By Tashinga

'The struggle is great,
But my love is greater.
The toll is taxing,
But my child you are worth it.'
These are the words of the woman who birthed, fed and
took care of me.
My earliest memories of her,
Abiding to the traditions of our culture, all while giving
me the greatest love and life any mother could ever give
or offer.
Filled with the heart and spirit of the continent.
She took care of me,
With the passion only a woman could engage.
A refuge, a rock, a teacher, a mother, a parent, a
foundation and a friend.
She was all of this and more!
And even in our darkest moments,
When the sweltering heat seemed to beat upon our door,
And stifled me to the point where I would almost
suffocate,
 And my tears dried in my eyes,
She was the rain, the cooling storm.
That brought me that relief from the harsh world.
I promised that I would be strong for her just as she had
been for me.
And even today,
As I traverse the world,
And see cultures and religions,
Great and wide,
There is no love that captures me,
Like the love of an African mother did.

*'I am a Mommy's boy, and I am proud to be called one, because
she has always been my only superhero and inspiration.'*

By Tasara

A silent night
It's a silent night
There is no light
It's a dark night
But is that right
It just might

I flip the switch
The light is on
The light is bright
The light is white
It's a bright white light
I begin to write
I write a poem
A poem of a night
A silent night

*I am Tasara. I don't see poetry as something you just read or
write: it's something more than you can imagine*

A Message To The Young Child
Hunayn (Infinity)

Hitting a brick wall everyday
Not knowing if you're going to sleep okay
No mother no father to show you the way
But dear orphan on the side of the road on a
cold winters' night
You are loved!
By all the people who help you
Even those who are not in your sight.

Your love is better than all the riches in the world.

So believe that you are the future president
You are the future lawyer

You are the future
So hear not the words of discouragement
You are the one who will change the entire world
With your wisdom and love
Because even though you have nothing
You will gain everything.

*'I am the funniest person I know and I love to spread love
because a smile is the best donation anyone can receive.'*

Roses
By Haneen

We're like roses , you and me
An orchestra in nature playing a beautiful symphony
Our roots deep in the ground
And thorns around our stem

These are our weapons that keep us safe and sound
We're like roses you and me
We have different colours to share
But be too quick to pick us

Oh then you'll be in despair

We're like roses you and me
Please do hear me out
We all begin low but finally stand tall and stout

We're like roses you and me
So many colours so vibrant

You have to believe in magic because
when you see a rose you'll fall into an enchantment

'I believe poetry is a drug.
I want everyone to be addicted.'

Mornings

By Lundi

The mornings,
Waking up,
I feel hazy,
My mind in a sea of confusion,
Searching for land on which to make sense of things; But
alas,
I almost drown in the sea of 'just one more minute'
Sooner or later however,
I always find myself landing on Weekend or Weekdays.

The Weekend island
The people there,
Very friendly,
Suffering from a virus called 'weekend madness' or
'happiness', Enjoy it is more like it

No shortages of smiles or pina coladas
Everyone is trying to rediscover something
Everyone is friendly and hopes that their time will never
end Their time,
However,
Flies by and passes like lightning.

The Weekday island
Sworn enemies and polar opposites to the Weekend
islanders

Epidemics running wild,
'Monday Blues', 'Early Mornings', 'wrong side of the bed'
and 'Do I have to';

They often put their pride to the side and retire to the
Weekend island for a cure,

An island in abundance of misery, agony and despair
with no shortages of booze

because everyone's trying to forget something

Everyone hates each other and can't wait for the day to
end so they can go home
Their time passes so slowly,
It feels and compares to a prison sentence.

Unfortunately,
I myself don't have a choice on which island to land For
the wind blows my sail

Poetic Dream

*'My name is Lundi and sometimes writing things down can be
easier than saying them out loud; at times the words flow like a
waterfall from my brain into my hands and are output as ink
and other times its like hunting for a turtle on land.'*

Message

Hello past, its future you. We need to talk . . .

Thank you for the pain you put me through.

The most beautiful diamonds are made in the highest to temperatures.

Your faith is strong, just take a leap! Like an ocean, your worth runs deep.

Don't let anyone use you. You are more that just a tool.

Free yourself!

For you are not a domesticated beagle. You soar great heights.

Spread your wings and unleash the eagle!

I know you've been facing difficulties . . . Don't let your rage get the best of you. Keep it away, put it in a cage.

Your courage is a mystery.

Your wisdom is a mastery.

I remember when I was you and you wished to be me ! The future you wanted to see,

Very soon, trust me, It'll be!

Never forsake your smile!

You glimmer like a dime!

My name is Vuyo. Judging by my poetry, I think a lot about the future. I'm anxious about what the future holds and it's something that gets me quite deep. So, poetry is my reinsurance and my energy outlet. Anyone else like that?

Bow Down

Let's bow down and give our thanks to those who declared us royalty.

To those who enthroned us and worshipped our happiness since our first breath,

For they tackle our never ending turmoil and seem to smile at the end of it.

Let's bow down to the scarifies they make and the bruises they take, just to make sure we awake to see the next sunrise.

Let's bow down to their restless nights and their restless might.

Let's bow down to your Fathers and Mother Grannies and Aunts,

Parents and Guardians,

Because through their sacrifices, we find life

By_.rockerfeller

BIOGRAPHIES OF POETS
AND TEACHERS

Palestine

In Palestine, the project is led by secondary school teacher, **Rania El Swalhir** and the poet is **Hind Zaqout**. Hind Zaqout studied Arabic Language at the University of Gaza and gained her teaching qualification in 2010. She also has qualifications in communication skills and constructive criticism.

Hind has taught Arabic language at the UNRWA schools in Gaza since 2007 and has taught creative writing since 2015. She led the poetry workshops for *Dream a Difference* in 2017 and we are delighted that she is continuing to work with the project this year. She is working with a group of secondary school children aged 12–14 years old.

Uganda

In Uganda, the project is situated in refugee camps and is led by the National Association of Social Workers in Uganda.

The artist working there is a songwriter and musician, **Hassan Kayemba**, who founded the Bitone Center for Children, located in the capital city of Kampala. The center is a music- based home that houses twenty-five children between the ages of 8 to 18, from every corner of Uganda. The program works with youth who have been traumatized by the death of their parents or loss of their home due to disease, war, or economic hardship. The full name of the center is actually Bitone Center for 'Disadvantaged' Children, but to me, their attitudes reflect the contrary. The joy the kids experience from performing and nurturing their talents seems to transcend any losses they have experienced.

Two Ugandan musicians/actors, Branco Sekalegga and **Hassan Kayemba**, founded the center in 2004, in an effort to combine their passion for the arts with their passion for social change. Bitone provides education, life-skills, physical care, mental healthcare as well as a thorough understanding of traditional Ugandan music, theatre and folklore.

United Kingdom

In the UK, the project is situated at two rural primary schools and two secondary schools.

Lucinda Jarrett is founder and director of Rosetta Life, an award-winning arts in health innovation charity, that enables people to write and perform stories that challenge the stigma and perception of illness, bereavement and loss. Rosetta Life runs the poetry project, *Dream a Difference*.

She also works with performance arts in neuro rehabilitation and leads the project Stroke Odysseys. Stroke Odysseys is a performance arts initiative in neuro- rehabilitation that improves the quality of life and reduces the anxiety and depression of people who are living with the effects of a stroke. The programme is delivered in hospital and community contexts and currently operates in London, Berkshire, Buckinghamshire and Bristol.

Lucinda works with movement, poetry and songmaking, theatre and opera. She is passionate about creating performances that forge strong and transformative relationships between audiences and performers and has been fascinated in how the Skype workshops have created strong connections between children and young people in differing cultures, economic, social and political circumstances. She is an eternal optimist and inherited a dangerous dreaming from her father, but hopes that her idealism is grounded in practical possibilities.

Lucinda lives in a small village in West Oxfordshire and worked at Chadlington Primary School and The Cotswold School for *Dream a Difference*.

Chris Redmond is a writer, performer and musician whose work often focuses on cross-media collaboration. A regular at UK music and literature festivals, he has performed on BBC Radio One, BBC Radio Four (*Bespoken Word* and *Pick of The Week*), Sky Arts, BBC Scotland's *Culture Show* and recently on Scroobius Pip's XFM show *The Beatdown*.

Chris worked at Dartington Primary School with a group of children aged 9–11 years old.

Francesca Beard was born in Malaysia and grew up on an island balanced on the equator, surrounded by sea-eagles. She now exists as a London-based poet who has been called 'the Queen of British performance poetry' (*London Metro*) and 'spine-tingling' (*The Independent*) plus many other (less flattering) things. She has performed her poetry all over the world, from a shopping mall in Bangkok to a prison in Colombia, to New York's Nuyorican Café to Zimbabwe's National Library. She runs creative writing workshops with All Change, the Arvon Foundation, Apples and Snakes – and that's just the A's.

South Africa

Mutinta Bbenkele (*WordnSound*) is a spoken word artist based in Johannesburg South Africa. She is a *Tedx* Speaker as well as Global Citizen Performer. Having performed poetry for just over 9 years and having traveled extensively, Mutinta remains an active Arts Administrator with a love for teaching.

USA

Kirsten Casey has an MA in English and has been teaching local children poetry for over a decade, at school, in workshops and at poetry camps. She is a poet-teacher with California Poets in the Schools and teaches creative writing at Forest Charter School in Nevada City. She finds poetic inspiration from odd news stories, remarkable words, and the mysteries of the human body. Her first collection, *Ex Vivo: Out of the Living Body* was published by Hip Pocket Press in 2012, and she has another volume on the way.

Kirsten lives at the top of Banner Lava Cap Mountain, once a volcano. Her home is minutes from Scott's Flat Lake and less than an hour from the Yuba River in the South Yuba River watershed on the Western Slope of the Sierra.

Conrad Cecil has lived in London, Paris and since 2016, in California. In France, he founded *La Compagnie de la Tangente* under the patronage of award winning poet and playwright, Roland Dubillard (Moliere 2011 award), and performed in French at the Avignon Festival and on the Champs Elysees, in collaboration with German filmmaker Werner Schroeter. Conrad can be seen in historical dramas and contemporary thrillers alongside

Sophie Marceau, Liam Cunningham, Clémence Poésy, Johan Leysen and Moritz Bleibtreu. His book, *L'anglais Pour la Diffusion International du Spectacle*, is in French and English and focuses on performing arts production, and he has prepared a fine press edition of *Shakespeare's Sonnets* with Petrarch Press. He divides his time between Los Angeles and the Sierra Foothills, running workshops on performing poetry at Beyond Baroqueliterary arts center in Venice, and coaching poetry for both *Poetry Out Loud* and *Dream A Difference* at Nevada County Arts Council. He has a master's degree in Directing and Dramaturgy from the Royal Academy of Dramatic Art and King's College London.

Conrad and Kirsten worked in Nevada Country, California at two small rural schools entitled Grizzly Hill School and Washington School. They also worked with a musician at both schools.

Zimbabwe

Mildred Bosha is a social worker at Island Hospice Haraare and with bereaved children, aged 10–16 years old. She received mentoring from Lucinda Jarrett to lead the creative writing project which she begain in 2017. We are delighted that Island Hospice continues to be a partner in 2018.

Mildred is working on the hospice programme designed for young carers and bereaved children which is aimed at promoting loss adjustment, coping and resilience which in its turn, should reduce their vulnerabilities.

The *Dare to Dream a Difference* workshop is aimed at acknowledging and working with the children's challenges by providing a supportive environment for the children to express their feelings and to share experiences. The children come together and through play, drawings, poetry, letter writing and discussion were able to open up, share their experiences and to express their feelings.

Island Hospice continues to conduct psychosocial support activities for vulnerable children in their community, understanding that these programmes need to be an ongoing process towards healing.

Loice Majongwe delivered the project at another location: Prince Edward School, Harare, during 2018/19. Loice is married and a mother of two. She is a teacher by profession and teaches English language and literature.

Loice developed an interest in poetry and creative writing and teaches up to GCSE Level. She describes herself as a confident woman, who believes in exploring young minds and assisting them in developing their talents.